# SWEDISH AMERICAN GENEALOGY A[ND] SELECTED TITLES AT THE LIBRARY OF CONGRESS

Compiled and Annotated by
Lee V. Douglas

**CONTENTS**

| | |
|---|---|
| I. Introduction | 1 |
| II. General Works on Scandinavian Emigration | 3 |
| III. Memoirs, Registers of Names, Passenger Lists, Essays on Sweden and Swedish America | 5 |
| IV. Handbooks on Methodology of Swedish and Swedish-American Genealogical Research | 23 |
| V. Local Histories in the United Sates | |
|     California | 28 |
|     Idaho | 29 |
|     Illinois | 30 |
|     Iowa | 32 |
|     Kansas | 32 |
|     Maine | 34 |
|     Minnesota | 35 |
|     New Jersey | 38 |
|     New York | 39 |
|     South Dakota | 40 |
|     Texas | 40 |
|     Wisconsin | 41 |
| VI. Personal Names | 42 |

## I. INTRODUCTION

Swedish American studies, including local history and genealogy, are among the best documented immigrant studies in the United States. This is the result of the Swedish genius for documenting almost every aspect of life from birth to death. They have, in fact, created and retained documents that Americans would never think of looking for, such as certificates of change of employment, of change of address, military records relating whether a soldier's horse was properly equipped, and more common events such as marriage, emigration, and death.

When immigrants arrived in the United States and found that they were not bound to the single state religion into which they had been born, the Swedish church split into many denominations that emphasized one or another aspect of religion and culture. Some required children to study the mother tongue in Saturday classes, others did not. Some, more liberal than European Swedish Lutheranism, permitted freedom of religion in the new country and even allowed sects to flourish that had been banned in Sweden. Amidst all these schisms the

Augusta Synod in Rock Island, Illinois, remained the largest and most influential, the church that produced the most books and founded Augustana College in Rock Island, Illinois. In this city, and associated with the college, the Swenson Center is a repository of Swedish culture in America and a source of documents for genealogists (see more about this below).

Most immigrants adjusted well and became Americans proud of their Swedish descent. Many have contributed significantly to the betterment of the country. Two phenomena, however, differentiate Swedish-American studies from those of other immigrant groups.

First, there arose a "Swedish America," which was not entirely of either country. It was characterized by societies designed to keep immigrants together, and sometimes to isolate them from American influence. Swedish-language magazines and books were published, and immigrants were encouraged to live in communities of their own kind, partly to form mutual-aid societies, partly to prevent assimilation. Thus arose Swedish cities such as Lindsborg in Kansas (where the local college still presents a yearly musical performance of great beauty), Bishops Hill in Illinois, and Chisago Lake in Minnesota. In the great Chicago fire of 1871, the southern part of the city, dubbed "Swedetown" by other Chicagoans, was the first to burn, and approximately 200,000 Swedish immigrants were rendered homeless. Swedish America has generated many written records of inestimable value to the genealogist. As early as the 1840s, Swedish journalists and writers toured American Swedish communities to gauge the extent to which the mother culture was being preserved. Some were sympathetic, others were acerbically critical, but all of their writings shed light on Swedish American local history.

The second phenomenon is the rise of a literary genre that expressed distaste for the new country. Although published almost entirely in Sweden rather than in America by immigrants, this genre began early and extended at least until 1996. It presents the United States as an inhospitable country to which emigration should be discouraged. While it is not a major factor in Swedish American local history, it is a sufficiently important phenomenon to include here; this compiler has not seen its like for any other immigrant group represented on the shelves of the Library of Congress. It is indeed striking that some Swedish immigrants took offense at American individualism and informality from the moment they set foot on American soil, and some never grew accustomed to it. Being a highly literate people, they expressed their feelings in published works (see Benzendal, Johansson, and Kremer below for examples). Austin and Daun below, both of them Swedes writing for Swedes, discuss Swedish thought and possible causes for this attitude.

The genealogist and the historian are particularly fortunate because many of the records they need to consult are available in the United States. While this compiler does not normally mention Internet sites because of their notorious instability, two having to do with the subject are sufficiently noteworthy to deserve inclusion. The site www.familysearch.org provides online abstracts of vital records, and the Swenson Center at Augustana College in Rock Island, Illinois, possesses and sells microfiches of many whole records. These microfiches are not available online. The Center's site is at www.augustana.edu/administration/swenson. A vast project is being carried out in Ramsele, Sweden, to put ancient records on fiche, and many of these fiches are available through the Swenson Center. Further information may be obtained from their Website.

## II. GENERAL WORKS ON SCANDINAVIAN EMIGRATION

Augustana Swedish Institute. Yearbook--Augustana Swedish Institute. [Rock Island, Ill.], 1962/63- .

E184 .S23 A84a

The volume for 1962-1963 contains "Poet in Swedish America" ( pp. 7-11), an article by Arthur Landfors, "Augustana Church Archives" (pp. 12-14), describing the Augustana Lutheran Church's records and manuscript archives beginning in 1860; and "Augustana and the Printed Word" (pp. 15-30) by Victor E. Beck, describing books published by the Augustana Lutheran Church, many of them dealing with immigration and settlement.

The volume for 1963-1964 contains "Recollections of a Childhood and Youth by an Immigrant" (pp. 3-15) by O. Fritiof Ander of Gendalen near Gothenburg, and "In a Time of Language Transition" (pp. 38-46) by D. Verner Swanson, describing in some detail the experiences of first and second generation Swedish Americans in making the transition from Swedish to English. This article is particularly interesting because it does not present Swedish speakers as a unified group, but tells how attitudes and experiences differed with individuals and groups around the country. It provides a window through which to see how it felt to be an immigrant faced with the necessity of changing languages.

Volumes for 1964-1965 contain "Why Major in Swedish?" (pp. 3-7), by Corrine Keeffe; "My Summer in Scandinavia" (pp. 21-24), by Christina Benson, describing visits to relatives the author had never met; and "Language in Exile" (pp. 25-41), by Nils Hasselmo, describing the Swedish language as a literary medium and its fate in America.

75644317

*From Scandinavia to America: proceedings from a conference held at Gl. Holtegaard.* Byhistorisk arkiv for Sollerod kommune. Edited by Steffen Elmer Jorgensen, Lars Scheving, and Niels Peter Stilling. [Odense]: Odense University Press, 1987. 377 p. Ill., maps, bibliography for each paper.

E184. S18F75 1987

Twenty-one papers studying causes and effects primarily of Danish emigration, with a general history of the movement as well as case studies of Lolland-Falster, Mon, and Sollerod. Transportation of emigrants is described. Settlement and assimilation in the Midwest includes personal letters, changes in emigrants' language habits, six studies of the Scandinavian press in North America, and efforts to preserve Danish-American history.

88114767

Hasselmo, Nils. *Swedish America: an introduction.* New York: Swedish Information Service, 1976. 70 p., [4] leaves of plates, ill., bibliography. "Parts of this volume are based on chapters in Nils Hasselmo, Amerikasvenska."

E184 .S23 H33

An overview. Includes chapters on background and course of emigration; Swedish American religious, educational, and secular institutions; press, theater, and the use of the Swedish language in America; Swedish Americans prominent in politics, economics, education, research, and the

arts; Swedish Americans in the Civil War; Swedish America as of the date of publication.
76015850

Hildebrand, Karl Emil, ed. *Svenskarna i Amerika; populär historisk skildring i ord och av svenskarnas liv och underbara öden i Förenta Staterna och Canada.* Stockholm, A.-b. Historiska förlaget, [1924]. Front. illus. incl. maps, facsims., plates (part col.) ports., diagrs.

E184 .S23 H5

Beginning with Erik the Red's exploration of Greenland and Leif Eriksson's explorations in America, this book represents the cooperative effort of Swedish and Swedish American scholars to describe history and everyday life (as the title says, "popular historical description in word and picture") in the long saga of Swedish migration westward. Lavishly illustrated, the table of contents includes a list of illustrations for each of the twenty-four chapters, as well as a final list of illustrations in color, all of which are a treasure trove for the researcher seeking to visualize immigrant life in the various time periods. Each chapter is written by a different specialist, and the chapters on nineteenth- and twentieth-century North America cover states county-by-county, naming Swedes who settled there, their origins, and their families. No index.
25018688

Nelson, Olof Nickolaus, ed. *History of the Scandinavians and successful Scandinavians in the United States.* 2d. rev. ed. 2 vols. in 1. Minneapolis, Minn.: O. N. Nelson & Company, 1900. Plates, ports.

E184 .S18N42

Essays that tell the story of Scandinavian Americans from the earliest Norse voyages to the date of publication, although only Norwegians, Danes, and Swedes are included. The social life, churches and synods, educational institutions, and individual settlements are treated in considerable detail, with many individuals' names mentioned. Churches are particularly well represented, and their histories discussed in detail. There is an index of biographies included in this book, an index of portrait photographs, and a thirty-page annotated bibliography of Scandinavian historical literature in America. The latter includes biographies, county histories, histories of educational and other institutions, tours of Scandinavian settlements in America, ethnic newspapers, and collections of advertisements for Scandinavian American businesses.
00927

*Nordics in America: the future of their past.* Edited by Odd S. Lovoll. (Northfield, Minn.: Norwegian American Historical Association, 1993). xii, 228 p. Ill., bibliography for each paper.

E184 .S18N58 1993

Papers by seventeen specialists on the Scandinavian experience in America, viewing past events as they have shaped the present and will influence the future. They include history of Danes, Norwegians, Swedes, and Finns in North American education and art, reviews of published history of these groups, preservation of ethnic identity, literary representations, immigrant letters from America, letters sent from Denmark to immigrants in America, and formal efforts to preserve the American Scandinavian heritage.
93184685

Norman, Hans, and Harald Runblom. *Transatlantic connections: Nordic migration to the New World after 1800.* (Oslo: Norwegian University Press. Distributed world-wide excluding Scandinavia by Oxford University Press, [1988?]. 335 p. [9] p. of plates (1 fold.), ill. (some col.), bibliography.

JV6704 .N67 1988

An analysis of causes of migration within and from Iceland, Norway, Sweden, Denmark, and Finland, including patterns of movement and settlement in America. These studies make clear the considerable differences in the migration movements of the four Nordic nations, describing the phenomenon by country and by regions within each country and describing the effects that settlement in new lands had on each group. "America" as used in this work comprises Canada, the United States, and Latin America, and includes both urban and rural settlement. Aspects of immigrant life studied are agriculture, commerce, religion, labor and trade unions, language maintenance, and a unique chapter on immigrant authors and "literary careers on two continents."

End material includes an eight-page overview of research on emigration from Nordic countries, statistics on Nordic-born immigrants to Canada, the United States, and Australia by province and state, a list of administrative areas in the four Nordic countries illustrated by a foldout map, and an eighteen-page bibliography. Regions and towns in which immigrants settled in the United States and Canada are listed and many described in detail. Immigrants who became famous are listed. Statistical tables give numbers of Swedish emigrants by year and by parish. The final chapter gives suggestions for further study.

89130346

## III. MEMOIRS, REGISTERS OF NAMES, ESSAYS ON SWEDEN AND SWEDISH AMERICA

Ander, O. Fritiof (Oscar Fritiof). *The cultural heritage of the Swedish immigrant; selected references.* [Rock Island, Ill., Augustana College Library, 1956]. xix, 191 p.

Z1361 .S9 A55

A bibliography of sources that deal "with the immigrants who were conscious of an immigrant status, a feeling which gave rise to a desire to . . . perpetuate certain ideals and institutions in America. Thus references to such persons as Greta Garbo, Ingrid Bergman . . . are not included. [p. xi]." Most of the works listed were found in the Royal Library, Augustana College, Bethel College in St. Paul, Minnesota; North Park College, Chicago; the Swedish Methodist Historical Library, Evanston, Illinois; the Minnesota State Historical Society, St. Paul; Bethany College, Gustavus Adolphus College, and Uppsala College. Works are listed in ten categories: 1. Bibliography of bibliographies (pp. 1-10). 2. Background of Swedish emigration (pp. 10-24). 3. America books (pp. 24-36). 4. Emigrant guide books (pp. 36-46). 5. Swedish immigrants in American life, general contributions (pp. 46-75). 6. Church and education (pp. 75-113). 7. Religious and secular literature (pp. 113-33). 8. Art, music and the theater (pp. 133-47). 9. Newspapers, periodicals, and annuals; religious and secular (pp. 147-88). 10. Archive materials (pp. 188-91). Many collections of letters and other manuscript items by individuals are included.

Each section has a brief introduction, and works are listed alphabetically by author or title; none are annotated. No index.
 57000747

Arnstberg, Karl-Olov. *Svenskhet: den kulturförnekande kulturen.* [Stockholm]: Carlsson, [1989]. 387 p.

DL639 .A77 1989

 A scholarly study of the historical reasons for the characteristics of modern Swedes. Pages 214-54 give the history of Swedish rule in Finland, its diminution, and the resulting Finnish participation in the rule of their own country.
 89209164

Atterling, Carl. *Genom ekluten i Amerika.* Stockholm, A.V. Carlsons bokförlags-aktiebolag [1910]. 2 pl., 168 p.

E184 .S23 A7

 A Swedish author visits Swedish Americans in New York and New Jersey, Wisconsin, Minnesota, and the Dakotas. He stays in the homes of Swedish American families and describes life as he sees it through European eyes. Written for his countrymen back home, the book gives insights into daily life in the first decade of the twentieth century, as well as the Scandinavian's view of how emigrants and their descendants have fared in their new world.
 37019255

Austin, Paul Britten. *On being Swedish: reflections towards a better understanding of the Swedish character.* London, Secker & Warburg, 1968. [8], 182 p.

DL639 .A85 1968

 Written by a Swede for Swedes, this work may also explain to Americans the negative reaction of some immigrants to the new world. Austin writes, ". . . the Swede . . . assumes that reality can be made to behave." [p. 43] "In a society so devoted to its own perfection criticism becomes the national sport." [p. 21] For additional insights, see Arnstberg above, and Blanck and Dalin below. The book includes one untitled song by Carl Michael Bellman (1740-1795). [p. 118.]
 71384744

Barton, H. Arnold (Hildor Arnold). *A folk divided: homeland Swedes and Swedish Americans, 1840-1940.* Uppsala: Uppsala University; Stockholm: Distributor, Almqvist & Wiksell International, 1994. xv, 403 p. Ill., bibliography, index.

E184 .S23B27 1994b

 One out of every five Swedes emigrated between 1840 and 1940. This caused those at home to consider the reasons that had impelled their neighbors and relatives to leave and created "a complex love-hate relationship" [p. xi] between them. The emigrants, on the other hand, while maintaining a nostalgic memory of the homeland, often resented economic and political conditions that they felt had forced their departure and embraced the broader opportunities open to them in America. An entire literary genre arose based on the preservation of the Swedish ethnic identity abroad. Scholars and journalists traveled to America to assess the situation of emigrants. Swedish

Americans wrote on the same subject and were often critical of elements in Swedish society that were not obvious to those who had not lived abroad. This book discusses the subject in detail, beginning with the period 1840-1902 and chapters such as "A New Sweden Across the Sea," "The Creation of a Swedish American Identity," and "What Was Sweden To Do?" Part two covers 1903-1917 and "The Homeland Faces Its Emigration Crisis," "The Anti-Emigration Movement," and "The Heyday of Swedish America." Part three covers 1917-1940 and "A Changing Sweden and the Swedish Americans," "Travelers From Afar," on Swedish travelers' views of America after World War I, and "The Afterglow," on the depression years and the imposition of immigration quotas. Five-page essay on sources discussing principle works.
  95152978

Beijbom, Ulf. *Amerika, Amerika!: En bok om utvandringen.* Stockholm: Natur & Kultur, 1977. 263 p. Ill.
                                                                     E184 .S23 B319

The author is the director of the Utvandrarnas Hus and presents a detailed history of Swedish emigration to North America, pointing out that by 1900 every seventh Swede was living in the western hemisphere, and Chicago had the second largest urban Swedish population in the world. The book is illustrated with two hundred and forty photographs and drawings from the collection of the Emigrantinstitut and contains a three-page index of place names in Sweden, Canada, and the United States and a three-page personal name index. Brief bibliographies are included for each subject treated. Chapters present studies of political and economic circumstances in Sweden that encouraged emigration, and studies by time periods from the founding of Nya Sverige on the Delaware River in 1638 to the 1970s. The chapter "Transatlantiskt perspektiv" explains American circumstances, such as the American Revolution, that made the United States attractive to emigrants ("the pull") and European circumstances, such as the potato famine, that made Europeans want to leave ("the push"). "Emigrationen som industri" describes specifically how emigrants arranged their travels and the circumstances in which they traveled, how shipping lines, railroads, and land companies helped and prospered, how immigrants found land and bought it, and what they found when they arrived.
  77579321

Beijbom, Ulf. *Utvandrarna och Svensk-Amerika.* Stockholm: LT, 1986. 253 p. Ill., bibliography, index.
E184.S23 B323 1986

A history of Swedish emigration to and settlement in America from the 1840s by Ulf Beijbom, director for twenty-five years of the Emigrantinstitut in Växjö, with much information from the archives of that institution. The book begins with discussion of well-known immigrants and conversations with some of them during the author's travels in America. There follow sections on Swedish settlement in Minnesota, Chicago, and the plains states with three maps marking settlements, a description of Liverpool, England, the "stopping-off point" for emigrants, organizations in America that provided places for immigrants to congregate and to seek support, and a chapter on the Swedish press in America. Information on organizations and newspapers is particularly detailed, with names of groups and publications, locations, and dates when they were

active. Describes what it was like for emigrants who had to buy tickets, leave home, settle on the new continent, and make a go of it. Many illustrations of people, buildings, newspapers, and other publications.
   86215404

Benson, Adolph B., and Naboth Hedin; foreword by Carl Sandburg. *Americans from Sweden*. Benson [and] Naboth. Philadelphia, Lippincott, 1950 [1949]. 448 p. Bibliography follows each chapter, index.

E184 .S23 B328

   From poor immigrants to Americans of substance and influence, this book aims to describe "how this rise of the Swedes in America has come about . . . . In a sense, the book is a continuation of *Swedes in America*." [p. 11]. The development of this group is studied in four parts with thirty-five subcategories: Part I, Historical Background. "Colonization and Trade" and "Early Cultural Relations" covers the period from 1638 to the formation of the United States. "A State Creates the Swedes" takes the subject to the time of this book's publication in 1949. Part II, Religious Life, treats the complex religious movements among immigrants, with separate sections for Methodists, Episcopalians, Lutherans, Baptists, Mormons, and the Mission Friends. Part III, Denominational Education, describes in detail the histories of Augustana College, Gustavus Adolphus College, Bethany College, Luther College, Uppsala College, North Park College, and Bethel College and Seminary. Part IV, American Activities, discusses Swedes who achieved notoriety as lawyers, public officials, architects and builders, scientists, educators, health specialists, writers, musicians, actors, artists, industrialists, aviators and airplane builders, and businessmen, as well as sports, charities, and other organizations. The last eight pages are devoted to "The Character of Americans from Sweden."
   0005150

Benson, Adolph Burnett. *Farm, forge, and philosophy; chapters from a Swedish immigrant's life in America*. Chicago: Swedish Pioneer Historical Society, 1961. 162 p.

E184 .S23 B329

   The memoirs of Adolph Burnett Benson, a noted scholar on Swedish emigration and Swedish America. His published works are discussed in the introduction. The first forty-eight pages describe his life in Sweden during the 1880s and his voyage in steerage at about ten years of age, with his parents, to America and their processing through Ellis Island. On pages forty-nine through sixty-two he gives a first-hand account of the experiences of a child who spoke no English and began to attend school in Connecticut in the 1890s, comparing the "wild" [p. 60] behavior of American children to the discipline he remembered in Sweden, and giving vivid examples of linguistic difficulties that he encountered. He subsequently spent a long career teaching at Dartmouth and Yale. The book ends with his "A Retrospect in Retirement" at the age of seventy-eight.
   61004389

Benson, Adolph Burnett, and Naboth Hedin, ed. *Swedes in America, 1638-1938*. Published for the Swedish American Tercentenary Association. New Haven, Yale University Press; London, H.

Milford, Oxford University Press, 1938. xvi, 614 p. Front. plates, ports.

E184 .S23 B33

Written for the three hundredth anniversary of Swedish settlement in America, this book is intended to "recall by summaries and representative examples the roles played by Swedes as American pioneers and citizens" [editor's preface]. Thirty-five articles by different authors sum up Swedish activity under the following headings: colonists, colonial landmarks, the Swedish language in America, farmers, pioneers of the Northwest, geographical distribution, Swedish place names in America, religion, charities and self help, colleges, newspapers, writers in Swedish, magazines, authors, journalists, translations of Swedish literature, four representatives of the intellect (Arrhenius, Berzelius, Linné, Swedenborg), the new church, professors, public school educators, lawyers, public officials, doctors, gymnastics, sportsmen, inventors, engineers, architects and builders, composers, opera singers, The American Union of Swedish Singers, moving picture actors, stage and radio performers, painters and sculptors, soldiers and sailors, aviation, manufacturers, businessmen, imports and importers. Photographs of Johan Printz, Holy Trinity (Old Swedes) Church in Wilmington, Delaware, Johannes Hult, Tyve Nilsson Hasselquist, Carl Aaron Swensson, Ernst Teofil Skarstedt, Carl Sandburg, Selma Lagerlöf, Emanuel Swedenborg, Carl Emil Seashore, Johan August Udden, Agnes Samuelson, John Lind, the Lindberghs (father and son), Carl Arthur Hedblom, John Ericsson, Vincent Bendix, Ernst Frederik Werner Alexanderson, Howard Hanson, Jenny Lind, Warner Oland, Greta Garbo, Dorothy Peterson, Carl Milles, Captain George Fried, Major Erik H. Nelson, Colonel Charles A. Lindbergh, Francis J. Plym, George N. Jeppson, and G. Hilmer Lundbeck. Fifteen-page personal name index. Most articles are followed by short bibliographies. Articles contain detailed lists of names and locations of institutions and publications, with many statistics.

38027493

Benzendal, Johan. *Amerikanska brev*. Uppsala, J.A. Lindblad [1925]. 254 p.

E184 .S23 B38

Letters of Gösta Bookstedt to her brother in Stockholm and a tale of differences between American and Swedish culture. She and her brother have observed that Swedish-language newspapers from America print little news about current Swedish culture and politics, and they work out a plan for her to go to America and offer her services to one of the publications in order to remedy this fault. Certain of a warm reception, she begins a journey of revelation about America. Her first impression upon entering the offices of a New York newspaper is one of deep offense. The men in the room do not stand when she enters, their collars are unbuttoned, their neckties loosened, and some have their feet on their desks. Like so many Swedish writers before her, she has her first experience of American informality, and she does not approve. Unlike some, however, the plucky journalist persists in her intention to bring Swedish culture to Swedish America. She survives a blunt statement that Swedish Americans are not interested in Swedish books, which have to be ordered from Europe at great price, and she is told that Swedish politics will not sell newspapers in the United States. Her subsequent letters reveal more about Swedish than American thought as she explains these events to her brother, but she does not give up and eventually lands a position that takes her around the country to Swedish American communities where she stays with Swedish American families and reports on the communities' cultural affairs.

This in turn leads her to make often interesting observations about the two countries. Americans, she finds, are more ready to help one another and are deeply interested in invention; this is the key to America's emerging status as an industrial giant. Swedes, on the other hand, are more interested in philosophy and matters of the mind. Miss Bookstedt's letters end with an essay defining the kind of literature that edifies the reader and a suggestion that an effort to purge Swedish American reading of American detritus, such as detective novels, would go far toward maintaining an acceptable level of culture among her compatriots abroad.
37019265

Berger, V. (Vilhelm). *Svensk-amerikanska meditationer*. Rock Island, Ill., Författarens förlag, 1916. 151 p.
"Samtliga artiklar i denna bok hafva under de senaste åren varit synliga i svensk-amerikanska tidningar och tidskrifter." (Förord.)

E184 .S23 B4

Eighteen articles on Swedish American customs and attitudes. Berger discusses emigration, americanization, factionalism, relations between parents and children, condition of women, attitudes towards other ethnic groups, nature and importance of the Augustana Synod, Swedish American press, organizations, politics, culture, attitudes toward Sweden, opinions on the attempt to maintain a Swedish identity in the new world, and a largely successful attempt to compare objectively economic, social, and political conditions in the two countries.
37019242

Bergman, Carl Johan, and Fredrik Bergman. *Amerikabreven*. Utg. och kommenterade av Otto Rob. Landelius. Förord av Vilhelm Moberg. Stockholm: Natur och kultur [1957]. 235 p. Ills., ports., facsims., maps.

E84 .S23 B45

The brothers Carl Johan and Fredrik Bergman emigrated from Östergötland in 1879. Five days after their arrival in America they sent their first letter to their sisters in Sweden. The correspondence continued through 1928, covering half a century of news about their life and the lives of their countrymen in Texas. Letters averaged one per month, mentioned many names, and the publisher has added notes to clarify events and persons referred to. Photographs include the letter of September 9, 1879, from New York. Portrait photographs of Fred Bergman, Carl Johan Bergman, their sisters Sofie Johansson and Hanna Ekström, Johan Johansson, Maja Stina Persdotter, Anders Fredrik Wigander, Emma Gustafva Wigander, Eduard Andersson, Henric Carlson, Erik Gustaf Becker, Gotthard Wilhelm Wallén, Anna Lindblom, Alfred Andersson, Hulda Landström, Carl August Fornell, Theodor Ekström, Svante Gottfrid Svensson, Anna Elggren, Amanda Olson, Ernst W. Olson, and Ruth Hildegard. Other photographs and drawings include the farms where the brothers were born, the deck of the ship on which they traveled, a ship's ticket--or "passagerare-kontrakt"--for emigration, the brothers' store in Lund, Texas, Carl Johan Bergman's obituary in "Texas Posten" for February 19, 1903, his gravestone in Lund, the Swedish Lutheran Bethlehem Church in Lund, their farmhouse in Lund, the new store built by Fred in Elgin, Texas, just after his brother's death, and a newspaper advertisement for it. Four-page name index, two-page place and subject index, foldout map of Linköping (on one side) and the northeast corner of

Travis County, Texas, on the other. Five-page chronology of Swedish-Texan history.
a 58001200

Blanck, Dag. *Becoming Swedish-American: the construction of an ethnic identity in the Augustana Synod, 1860-1917.* Uppsala: Ubsaliensis S. Academiae. Distributed by Uppsala University Library, 1997. 240 p. Ill.

E184 .S23 B54 1997

A doctoral dissertation studying the influence of the Augustana Synod (the largest Swedish religious body in America) in the formation of Swedish America.
98116215

Blomé, Göran. *Twelve ways to the top: Swedish-American success stories.* [Translation by Victor Kayfetz]. New York: Swedish-American Chamber of Commerce; Sollentuna, Sweden: Blome Produktion, 1985. 207 p. Ill.

E184.S23 B55 1985

The stories of people who "have learned something from each bad experience" (p. 9). Written originally in Swedish, the book exemplifies the author's opinions concerning the resilience and the strengths of his countrymen. Many of the Swedish Americans here portrayed descend from families who "left Sweden with feelings of resentment toward the old country" (p. 5), but prospered in the new. Persons discussed are Rand Araskog, chairman of ITT, Frederick O'Green, Chairman of the Board of Litton Industries, Roy Anderson, chairman of Lockheed, Edward E. Carlson, chairman of United Airlines, Robert A. Swanson, head of Genentech, Erik Jonsson, chairman of Texas Instruments and three-time mayor of Dallas, Texas, Rudolph Peterson, president of the Bank of America, Robert O. Anderson, president of the Arco oil company, John W. Nordstrom, founder of the Nordstrom department store chain (in a chapter entitled "The Nordstrom Saga"), Franklin Forsberg, magazine publisher and U.S. ambassador to Sweden, Curtis Carlson, called "the Swedish king of Minnesota," head of Carlson Companies, Inc., and Peter and William Hoglund, called "the GM brothers" because of their high positions in General Motors.
86181595

Carlsson, Sten Carl Oscar. *Swedes in North America, 1638-1988: technical, cultural, and political achievements.* Stockholm, Sweden: Streiffert, 1988. 136 p. Ill., maps, ports.

E184 .S23 C37 1988

An overview touching on all the phases of immigration that are discussed in more detail in larger volumes. Points out that the Swedes were among the first European settlers (1638), preceded only by the British, French, Spanish, and Dutch. Swedish settlements in Delaware, Pennsylvania, and New Jersey, although lost to the Dutch by 1655, maintained contact with the mother country throughout the eighteenth century. The second wave, beginning in the 1840s, brought one and a quarter million people to America--approximately one of every five Swedes. The author states that "a sizeable part of modern Swedish achievement has taken place on the other side of the Atlantic from Sweden." [p. 8] He proceeds to describe both immigration and achievements. Photographs and drawings of individuals, groups, and buildings. Ten-page bibliography arranged under the following subjects: Swedish and Finnish colonists on the Delaware, Descendants of the colonists

of New Sweden, First Swedes in New York City, Swedes in the American war of independence, Mass emigration 1845-1930: the Swedish background, Swedes in North America: fundamental characteristics, Swedish settlements in North America: regional distribution, Local links between Sweden and North America, Farmers, Engineers, Transport activities, Building contractors, Big businessmen, Metalworks, carpenters, and cabinet-makers, Maidservants, and seamstresses, Those who disappeared, Pastors, Two mainstreams in Swedish American Culture: newspapers and organizations, Scientists, Writers, painters, and composers, Politicians. Two-page index of names of "permanent and temporary Swedish Americans."
88146845

*Clipper ship and covered wagon: essays from the Swedish pioneer historical quarterly.* Edited by H. Arnold Barton. New York: Arno Press, 1979. 255 p. in various pagings. Ill., notes, and list of Arno Press publications on Scandinavians in America.

E184 .S23 C55

Eighteen articles reprinted from the *Swedish Pioneer Historical Quarterly*. 1. The Emigrant Institute, Växjö, "The dream of America: pictures from an exhibition." 2. O. Fritiof Ander, "Reflections on the causes of emigration from Sweden." 3. John E. Norton, "Parson Baird, Bishop Hill, and Manifest Destiny." 4. Olof E. Olson, "A letter from one generation to another." 5. Ernst Ekman, "Wetterman and the Scandinavian Society of San Francisco." 6. George F. Erickson, "Letters to Linus." 7. Frederick Hale, "Nordic immigration, the new puritan?" 8. Tell G. Dahllöf, "Three Americans look at Sweden." 9. Emory Lindquist, "Appraisal of Sweden and America by Swedish emigrants: the testimony of letters in 'Emigrationsutredningen.'" 10. Michael Brook, "Radical literature in Swedish America: a narrative survey." 11. Sture Lindmark, "Re-immigration to Sweden from the United States." 12. Torvald Höjer, "Swedish emigration and the Americanization of Sweden: some reflections." 13. Conrad Bergendoff, "The Swedish immigrant and the American way." 14. Folke Hedblom, "The Swedish speech recording expedition in the Middle West." 15. Carl-Werner Pettersson, "From Brinkalid to sunrise--modern saga of discovery." 16. Todd Engdahl, "The fourth generation speaks." 17. Sten Carlsson, "Sweden and America after 1860: a research project." 18. Karl A. Olsson, "Dream of splendor." Some photographs. Some articles contain bibliographical notes. Appendix listing publications of the Swedish Pioneer Historical Society 1950-1978.
78014619

*Dalsländska emigrantbrev.* [Mellerud:] Vasaorden av Amerika, Logen Mellerud, 644 [1963]. 179 p. Ill., ports.

E184 .S23 D3

A collection of letters to and from emigrants from Dalsland. Although some of the correspondents are anonymous, most are known and information is given on their families, origins, and places of residence in America. Named correspondents are Carl P. Eriksson, Olle Strid, Zander Nilsson, J. F. Nilsson, J. A. Johansson, J. M. Bonggren, Emelia Anreasson, Simon Andersson, August Segerberg, H. Davis and A. Davidsson, Emelia Karlsson, and Jakob Swenson. Photographs of Hertha and August Segerberg, the Simon Andersson family, and O. A. Strid.
72252568

Daun, Åke, *Svensk mentalitet ett jämförande perspektiv*. 2. omarb. uppl. [2nd rev. ed.]. Stockholm: Rabén Prisma, 1994. 255 p.

DL639 .D38 1994

"In his book, *Det Svenska folklynnet* (The Swedish National Character), a by-product of the emigration study [in 1911], he [Gustav Sundbärg] regrets that Swedes seemed to find it remarkably easy to adapt to the great land in the West." [p. 2] of the English translation (see below). Daun proceeds to examine culture, personality, relations, feelings, rationality, melancholy, proverbs and mentality, the Sweetishness within, and the history of Sweetishness. See also Austin, Arnstberg, and Blanck above.

4211066

Daun, Åke, *Swedish mentality*. Translated by Jan Seeland; foreword by David Cooperman. Svensk mentalitet. English: University Park, Pa.: Pennsylvania State University Press, 1996. xii, 236 p.

DL639 .D3813 1996  Sweden

English translation of *Svensk mentalitet*.
95014585

*Det Barged vied Delaware: om svenska hembygder i Amerika*. [redaktör, Gunilla Linberg]. Stockholm: Riksförbundet för hembygdsvård, 1986. 168 p. Ill., bibliographies.

E184 .S23 B67 1986

Overview of Swedish traditions in America by twelve authors. Sten Carlsson, "Svensk invandring till Nordamerika." Robert W. Harper, "När Sverige skulle bli en världsmakt." Richard Hulan, "Historiska minnen i Delaware." Josef Rydén, "Big Belly på Printz Hall." Olov Isaksson, "Bishop Hill–det värdefullaste svenskminnet." Kerstin Brorson, "Museum och kulturcentrum i Philadelphia." Phebe Fjellström, "Svenska traditioner i Californien." Folke Hedblom, "Amerikasvenskarnas hemspråk" Karl A. Olsson, "Svensk fromhet i Amerika." Lilly och Lennart Setterdahl, "Selma i Chicago." Christopher Olsson, "Otaliga föeningar håller kulturarvet levande." Gunilla Lindberg, "Motbilder--emigrationen i nytt ljus."

Photographs: Timber workers in Washington state in the 1900s. The American Swedish Institute in Minneapolis. Selma Jacobson opening a time capsule found in a statue of Linné, which was an attraction at the Chicago World Fair of 1893. The statue itself. Selma Jacobson in the Chicago archive of Swedish American newspapers. Dalkullan Swedish Imports in Chicago. Gravestone of Lars Peter Bergmann, born Sweden 1820, died Cambridge, Minnesota, 1889. Hilmar colony's church, 1903, near Turlock, California. Anna Lundell as "melon festival queen" in Turlock, 1910. Liliane Johnson's house in Hilmar, California, 1907. "Höet Bärgas," (haymaking) and a view of Bishop Hill, black and white photos of paintings by Olof Krans. Statue and portrait of Johan Printz (called "Big Belly" because he weighed 400 pounds), first governor of Nya Sverige--the portrait hangs in the Swedish American Historical Museum in Philadelphia. The Morton Homestead in Essington, Pennsylvania. One of three old Swedish houses along Darby Creek, Pennsylvania. Holy Trinity "Old Swedes Church" in Wilmington, Delaware. St. Mary Anne's Episcopal Church, North East, Maryland. Drawing of an Indian family by Pehr Lindeström, Nya Sverige, 1653. A trade treaty with the Indians signed by Governor Printz. Early map of Nya

Sverige. Family of Swedish immigrants in front of their log cabin in Minnesota in the 1800s.
87147286

Hedblom, Folke. *Svensk-Amerika berättar*. [Stockholm]: Gidlund, 1982. 185 p. [8] p. of plates; ill., maps, index.

E184 .S23 H39 1982

   A report on three linguistic expeditions from 1962 to 1966 to study and record on tape Swedish dialects still spoken in North America. Expeditions went to Maine, Massachusetts, Connecticut, Rhode Island, New York, Pennsylvania, Ohio, Indiana, Illinois, Wisconsin, Minnesota, Iowa, Nebraska, Kansas, Colorado, Utah, Idaho, Oregon, Washington, British Columbia, Alberta, Saskatchewan, Virginia, Tennessee, Georgia, Alabama, Mississippi, Louisiana, Texas, and Oklahoma. Includes a map of the United States and southern Canada with Swedish settlements marked and smaller maps throughout the book showing single states or parts of states in more detail. Much oral history provided by the Swedish Americans interviewed and much comment on Swedish customs and architecture in the places visited. Many people are named in the text. Two-page subject index.
   82183364

Heffner, John H., comp. *The records of the Swedish Lutheran Churches at Raccoon and Penns Neck*. 2 vols. Topton, [Pa.]: J.H. Heffner, 1997.

F144 .R13 H44 1997

98218252

Hoflund, Charles J. (Charles John). *Getting ahead: a Swedish immigrant's reminiscences, 1834-1887*. Ed. by H. Arnold Barton. Carbondale: Southern Illinois University Press, 1989. xvi, 127 p. Ill.

E184 .S23 H564 1989

   The memoirs of Charles J. Hoflund, who, in 1850, at the age of fourteen, sailed with his family on the ship "Virginia" from Gothenburg, and two months later arrived at New York Fifteen well-chosen photographs and drawings show the Sweden that he left, a sister ship of the "Virginia," the South Street quay in New York where he disembarked, American sites and Swedish American groups of which he formed part. The family traveled to Albany, Buffalo, Chicago, and Rock Island, Illinois. The author took jobs as farmhand, errand runner for a saloon keeper, and finally as a lumberjack in Eau Claire, Wisconsin. Eventually he farmed, owned cattle, and participated in county politics. His willingness to express his feelings and the detail with which he describes everyday life in the 1850s and 1860s give the book the interest of a historical novel. Editorial notes for each chapter explain events and persons alluded to in the text.
   88030299

Hokanson, Nels Magnus. *Swedish immigrants in Lincoln's time*. Foreword by Carl Sandburg. First edition. New York, London: Harper & Brothers, 1942. xviii, 259 p. [23] leaves of plates; ill., ports, bibliography.

E184.S23 H6

Chapters on "Colonial Swedes on the Delaware," "Pioneer Swedes in America," "Swedish immigrants in Lincoln's time" (the overwhelming majority of Swedish Americans voted for and supported the policies of Abraham Lincoln), "Southern Swedes and forty-niners," "Prairie Swedes in Lincoln's Illinois," "Lincoln and the Swedish vote," "Swedes answer Lincoln's war appeal," "Swedish army officers who fought for Lincoln," "Swedish volunteers in the eastern regiments," "Swedish volunteers in western regiments," "Swedish sailors in Lincoln's service," "Swedes in the Confederacy," "Sweden and the Lincoln administration," and "Lincoln and the Swedes." Each chapter is followed by one to three pages of notes giving names of individuals and citing sources for further research. Sixty-eight illustrations, most of individuals or documents. Twenty-three appendices including a list of Swedes who fought in the Revolutionary War, towns and states in which subscribers to "Hemlandet" lived and number of subscribers in each town in 1855, names of Swedish students at Illinois State University 1851-1860, statement of an immigrant who had been lured into slave labor in 1866, a document for the care and employment of immigrant children in 1848, names of Swedish naval officers in the Civil War, Swedes in the Union Navy, Swedes from Massachusetts who enlisted during the Civil War, Swedish sailors in federal service who participated in the battle between the Monitor and the Merrimac, two first-hand descriptions of this battle, an excerpt from the memoirs of Gustaf Alstrand about Andersonville Prison, names of Swedish dead at Andersonville, Swedish officers in the Union Army, Swedes in Battery H First Illinois Artillery, Company D Fifty-seventh Illinois Infantry, Company C Forty-third Illinois Infantry, Company D Third Minnesota Infantry (The Scandinavian Company), other Swedish volunteers in Minnesota regiments, The Scandinavian Guards organized in Nicollet County, Minnesota, August 27, 1862, and volunteers from Iowa.
43001027

Holy Trinity Church (Wilmington, Del.). *The records of Holy Trinity (Old Swedes) Church, Wilmington, Del., from 1697 to1773*. Translated from the original Swedish by Horace Burr, with an abstract of the English records from 1773 to 1810. [Wilmington] Historical Society of Delaware, 1890. 772 p. Front.

F174 .W7 W73

01005961

Johansson, Anders. *Amerika: dröm. eller mardröm?* 2. uppl. Kalmar: A. Johansson, [1996] (Kalmar: KalmarSund). 235 p. Ill.

E184 .S23 J55 1996

*America, dream or nightmare?* weighs in solidly on the side of nightmare. Some immigrants were winners. Others were not. One regrets leaving Sweden because his sister there is rich, while he has nothing in America. Another fared better (pp. 41-72). A Norwegian (pp. 73-77) occupies a chapter entitled "Vi skulle ha stannat hemma allihop" [We should have stayed home]. A swedish immigrant (pp. 78-82) declares that there is more poverty in America than in any other country. Another (pp. 83-84) lives and associates with Swedes on the West Coast, and his opinion of Americans is not high. One, in nine lines, describes a life of sickness and poverty on a welfare check of one hundred dollars per month. One keeps a map of Sweden on the wall and yearns for home (p. 89). One (pp. 91-96) found poverty in America. One does not feel at home among

Americans. She knows that some Swedish women have married rich Americans, but finds that women are not respected in America. Another woman believes that she has fared well in America, but would have done it with less effort in Sweden. On a visit to Sweden a stranger asked her if it is true that Americans are so poor that they must eat at soup kitchens in the streets. She answers that it is true, she has seen it many times from her window. A third woman grew up in New York. She visited relatives in Sweden and found the Swedes very likeable, but she did not like their apparent belief that Americans are rich. She returned to America and eventually left New York for Seattle, where she found many Swedish Americans and is happier. The book goes on with many statements of unhappiness in America, and articles on Scandinavian-American settlements. An indictment of the economics of the Reagan administration and of America in general, the book includes photographs showing luxury followed by squalor that by implication underlies it. A homeless man stands in front of Seattle's Millionaires' Club. A majestic city skyline is fronted by a closeup of a building with scabrous walls and windows broken or boarded up. Photographs from the nineteenth century show urban immigrants living in squalor. There are photographs of Hoovervilles in the 1930s and homeless men in the 1980s.
   97132551


Johnson, Amandus. *Swedish contributions to American freedom, 1776-1783.* 2 vols. Philadelphia, Swedish Colonial Foundation, 1953-57. Ills., ports., fold. maps, facsims., bibliography in each volume.

E184 .S23 J62  pt. 7, etc.

   Subtitled "Including a sketch of the background of the Revolution together with an account of the engagements in which Swedish officers participated and biographical sketches of these men" [title page] sums up the work in brief. Volume one (695 pages) describes the war, and volume two (466 pages) presents biographies of officers. Most of the latter are less than one page and are arranged by the nations for which the officers served (United States, England, France, Netherlands), with a separate listing for those of "uncertain" loyalty. Within these sections, names are listed alphabetically, with a comprehensive name index at the end of each section.
   53003581


Kræmer, Henry von. *Ur frihetslandets järnkäftar; en svensk emigrants erfarenheter i U. S. A.* Stockholm, Aktiebolaget Ljus [1914]. 3 p.l., 207 p.

E184.S23 K7

   A cautionary tale for Swedes considering emigration, "Out of the iron jaws of the land of freedom" is the epic of an emigrant named Erik who does not fare well in his new country. From the tedious hours at Ellis Island, where he hears horror stories of emigrants confined in cells for weeks, to the coast of California, where he considers drowning himself, he learns to abhor all things American. He finds a society that he despises for its emphasis on work and money, although he frequently complains that he has neither, an "orange-society" that sucks a man dry and throws him away. He holds many low-paying jobs, dislikes American food and suffers from the weather--hot and sweaty in New York, sweltering or freezing in the West. He suffers "the American disease," neuresthenia, but finds the hospitals fit only for setting broken bones. He finds that Americans, from doctors to factory workers, are uninterested in matters of the mind. He

describes a remarkable cross-country journey, during which he earns his living as a factory worker (he dislikes American workers for their unedifying conversation), a cowboy (he finds the cowboys cruel to animals and foreigners), and an assistant to a physician of doubtful origin and practice. In Yuma, Arizona, penniless but frantic to escape the heat, he meets a Norwegian immigrant of many years (a one-legged victim of the iron jaws) who tells him how to ride the rails to California. After a harrowing journey in and beneath the hurtling freight cars, he stands in the rising tide of the Pacific Ocean and considers whether death in the Pacific is preferable to life in America.
40025526

Lagevik, Elsa. *The people of the Red Barns: emigrants from Västmanlands, Kopparbergs, Gävleborgs, Västernorrlands, Jämtlands, Västerbottens, and Norrbottens län, 1851-1863 = De Röda Ladornas folk.* Translation in English by Vicky Oliver. Ockelbo, Sweden: E. Lagevik, [1996]. 328 p. Ill., maps.

E184 .S23 L34 1996

A continuation of the passenger information 1820-1850 by Olsson, below. The first part, in Swedish and English, describes the methods of obtaining passage, conditions during the voyage, and arrival in America, all illustrated with abundant, detailed drawings. The passenger information, however, must be sought out through the indexes, and these are complex to use. Because of this difficulty the compiler will describe the process necessary when the researcher has the book in hand.

Finding the Person:
1. There are three indexes contained on pages 251–322. They are by surname, by given name, and by date of birth; any of the three will lead to the individual sought.
2. As an example, turn to page 282 and look at lastname2 "Swing," followed by lastname1 "Persdotter," given name "Christina," born 1835-12-11, parish "Hassela," "family 51, :02."
3. To find Ms. Swing, the PARISH name is the key (Hassela). The index does not tell us in which "län" Hassela is located. One must go to the lists between pages 115-233 and look for the parish under each "län." Within the listings for each "län," the parishes are arranged alphabetically, and we find that Hassela parish is in "Gävleborgs län" on pages 164-170. Harking back to the information in the index (see number 2 above), Ms. Swing is listed in family number 51, and she is the second person listed under "Swing." Here we find all the information given in the index, as well as her place of birth, place of residence, relationship or occupation, the ship on which she sailed, and her passenger number on the ship.

Finding the Ship:
4. If one wishes information on the ship and who else sailed on it with Ms. Swing, we know from the parish record on page 167 that she sailed on the *Luleå*.
5. Go to page 325 where all the ships' names are listed and look up this name. It is found on pages 244 and 247. We know from page 167 that her passenger number was "94." She is listed as "Christina, Persdotter, Hassela, 51 :01." Her ship arrived in New York on August 20, 1858, and the other Swedish passengers on that voyage are also listed.

97156743

Landelius, Otto Robert. *Swedish place-names in North America.* Translated by Karin Franzén, edited by Raymond Jarvi. Carbondale Southern Illinois University Press, 1985. xvii, 372 p. Ill., bibliography, index.

E155 .L36 1985

Etymological/historical explanations of place names arranged by U.S. state and Canadian province. Names are alphabetically arranged within each section. Length of explanations ranges from two lines to two pages. Twenty-six pages of notes are also arranged by state and province.
84014192

Lundqvist, Jan. *Från Piteå till Piteo: när Amerikafebern nådde Pitebygden.* ABF Piteåbygden, 1992. 234 p. Ill.

E184 .S23 L86 1992

A pastiche of articles, photographs, and brief biographies of individuals and families from the part of Norrbotten around the coastal city of Piteå on the Gulf of Bothnia. Although much valuable information is contained in this first, 154-page part of the book, there is no name index for it. However, pages 156-224 are parish registers from Piteå, Horlax and Norrfjärden listing families by surname and giving year and place of birth, year of emigration, year of return to Sweden when appropriate, and profession. In cases when more than one family member is listed, family relationships are indicated. Years covered are 1840-1940.
94152429

Måwe, Carl Erik. *Värmlänningar i Nordamerika. Sociologiska studier i en anpassningsprocess. Med särskild hänsyn till emigrationen från Östmark.* [Säffle, Säffle tidn:s tr.], 1971. 339, 322 p. Ills.

E184 .S23 M23

Study and history of the adaptation of immigrants from Östmark to conditions in North America. American centers of settlement are studied historically, and Swedish settlers are named. Places discussed are Wisconsin; Chicago; in Minnesota, the city and county of Carver, the area around Karlslund-Buffalo, Moores Prairie, Cokato, Dussel, Collingwood, North Crow River, Knapp, Ostmark, Birchdale, Wheaton, and Minneapolis and St. Paul; in North Dakota, Wilton and Sheyenne; in Montana, Helena; in Idaho, Mullan and Troy; in Washington, Spokane, Seattle, Everett, and Klickitat; in Oregon and British Columbia, Portland and Vancouver; in Colorado, Denver and its environs. Some photographs and much statistical, biographical, and genealogical information but no name index. The last three hundred and twenty-one pages list immigrants from Östmark for the years 1852-1936. Listing is chronological and for each immigrant tells year, month, and day of emigration, profession, birthplace if other than Östmark, place of residence within the Swedish parish, last known place of residence in America, date of death or date of return to Sweden. For families, family relationships are indicated for each member.
73319892

Minotty, Paul, comp. *The records of Trinity Episcopal Church (Old Swedes), Swedesboro, Gloucester County, New Jersey, 1785-1975.* Woodbury, N.J.: Gloucester County Historical

Society, 1979. x, 475 p.

F144 .S976 M56

074662

Moberg, Vilhelm. *Den okända släkten*. Stockholm, Bonnier [1950]. 138 p.

E184 .S23 M6

Articles by Moberg, written for the people back home while the author still lived in America. Although Moberg's historical facts were sometimes questioned, and his attitudes toward America and Sweden changed through the years, this edition expresses a basic optimism about the Swedish immigrant experience. The "okända släkten" refers to Sweden's unknown relatives in America and their contribution to America's diversity and sense of freedom.

50039110

Moberg, Vilhelm. *Den okända släkten*. [Ny utg.] Stockholm, PAN/Norstedt, 1968. 150, (2) p.

E184 .S23 M6 1968

Moberg returned to Sweden in 1955. He had become disillusioned with America and recognized his personal inability to adapt to aspects of the country that he found repulsive, such as materialism and violence, and especially the fanatical mccarthyism that swept the land in the early 1950s. The Vietnam war caused him to add a chapter that further expressed this feeling.

70375858

Moberg, Vilhelm. *The emigrants*. Translated from the Swedish by Gustaf Lannestock, with a new introduction by Roger McKnight. St. Paul: Minnesota Historical Society Press, 1995. xxxiii, 366 p. Bibliography, pp. xiii-xxv.

PT9875 .M5 U713 1995

95015848

Moberg, Vilhelm. *Invandrarna*. Stockholm: Bonnier, 1972. 489 p.

PT9875 .M5 I6 1972

75535824

Moberg, Vilhelm. *The last letter home*. Translated from the Swedish by Gustaf Lannestock, with a new introduction by Roger McKnight. St. Paul: Minnesota Historical Society Press, 1995. xxxii, 230 p. Bibliography, pp. xxvii-xxix.

PT9875 .M5 S513 1995

95015845

Moberg, Vilhelm. *Nybyggarna*. Stockholm: Bonnier, 1975. 534 p.

PT9875 .M5 N9 1975

75535822

Moberg, Vilhelm. *The settlers*. Translated from the Swedish by Gustaf Lannestock, with a new introduction by Roger McKnight. St. Paul: Minnesota Historical Society Press, 1995. xxix, 399 p.

Bibliography pp. xxvii-xxix.

95015948

PT9875 .M5 N913 1995

Moberg, Vilhelm. *Sista brevet till Servige; romanen om utvandrarna*. Stockholm, Bonnier, [1959] . 366 p.

60019985

PT9875 .M5 S5

Moberg, Vilhelm. *The unknown Swedes: a book about Swedes and America, past and present.* Translated and edited by Roger McKnight, with a foreword by H. Arnold Barton. Carbondale: Southern Illinois University Press, 1988. xxviii, 182 p.

E184 .S23 M613 1988

This is an English translation of *Okända släkten*. It includes all chapters of the 1968 Swedish edition, including the final chapter on Vietnam, and thirty additional pages of notes for English-speaking readers. The notes are arranged by chapter and serve also as a bibliography for further reading.

88001731

Moberg, Vilhelm. *Unto a good land*. Translated from the Swedish by Gustaf Lannestock, with a new introduction by Roger McKnight. St. Paul: Minnesota Historical Society Press,1995. xxvii, 371 p. Bibliography.

95015847

PT9875.M5 I613 1995

Moberg, Vilhelm. *Utvandrarna*. Stockholm: Bonnier, 1972. 443 p. The first vol. of Moberg's tetralogy, *Romanen om utvandrarna*; the subsequent vols. are *Invandrarna, Nybyggarna*, and *Sista brevet till Sverige*.

PT9875 .M5 U7 1972

This first of Moberg's four-volume epic is about a Swedish family that emigrates to America. The novel shows conditions in Sweden that led to the decision to emigrate, the preparations for the journey, how the family made travel arrangements, conditions during the voyage, what they found when they disembarked, what they faced as they headed inland by various means of transportation, how they coped with a new language, new landscapes, new laws, new dangers. Informative for those who wish to know the everyday details of the immigrant experience. Following these four entries are listings for volumes of an English translation.

75535823

Nelson, Helge. *The Swedes and the Swedish settlements in North America*. 1943. Reprint. New York: Arno Press, 1979. 441, 73 p. Ill.

E184 .S23 N35 1979

Extremely detailed account of Swedish settlements in North America, giving names of settlers in order of arrival, listing family houses built or houses abandoned but still standing, telling trades

and professions, businesses and their owners, families of business owners, politics in the settlements, relationships with other settlements and with non-Swedish groups. Traces the process of adaptation to circumstances in each settlement. Places studied are New York City, New York state, New Jersey, Pennsylvania, New England, Ohio, Michigan, Wisconsin, Illinois with special sections on Chicago, Bishop Hill, and Rockford, sixty pages on Minnesota, Iowa, Kansas, Missouri, Nebraska, and Texas. Smaller sections study the mountain states, southern states, and Pacific states and Swedish settlement in Canada. Seven pages on linguistic transition. Each chapter is followed by copious bibliographical and explanatory notes. Extensive bibliography at end of volume one. Index of subjects, place names, and personal names. Volume two, bound together with volume one in this edition, is an atlas that gives cartographic information on all material covered in volume one.
78015197

Norelius, Erik. *De svenska luterska församlingarnas och svenskarnes historia i Amerika.* 2 vols. [n.p.], 1890-1916. Ill., index.

E184 .S23 N8

 Articles on settlers and pastors 1841-1854, with twenty-three pages on Bishop Hill. Development of the church in America to 1860: Iowa, with pastor M. F. Håkanson; in Illinois Andover and Berlin with pastors L. P. Essbjörn and Jonas Swensson; Galesburg and Knoxville with pastors T. N. Hasselquist and Håkan Olson; Moline, Rock Island, and Geneseo with pastor O. C. T. Andrén; the Immanuelsförsamlingen in Chicago with pastor Erland Carlsson; St. Charles, Geneva, and De Kalb; Rockford and Pecatonica with pastors A. Andrén and G. Peters; Princeton with pastor John Johnson; new settlements and churches in Indiana; Jamestown, New York; Sugar Grove (Hesse Valley), Pennsylvania; first settlements and churches in Minnesota; Chisago Lake with pastors P. A. Cederstam and C. A. Hedengran; St. Paul, Taylor's Falls, Rusheby, Vasa, and Red Wing; Stockholm, Wisconsin, with P. C. Borèn; Spring Garden, Cannon River, and Cannon Falls with pastor P. Beckman; Carver County, Götaholm, and Scandea with pastor P. Carlson; St. Peter and Scandian Grove with pastor J. Pehrson; Vista and Waseca County in Minnesota; other settlements where no Swedish congregations had been organized by 1860, including Wisconsin, Minnesota, Iowa, Michigan, Illinois, Indiana, Kansas, New York, and the cities of Boston and Brocton, Massachusetts. Volume one concludes with documents and additional notable persons associated with the churches. Volume two describes the activities of the Augustana Synod nationwide up to the twentieth century, with detailed lists of activities and names of individuals. Volume one contains many drawings of places and people; volume two contains photographs of most pastors and institutions mentioned.
02008188

Olsson, Nils William. *Swedish passenger arrivals in New York 1820-1850.* Stockholm, PA: Norstedt & Söners Förlag, 1967. 391 p. Ills. (part colored), facisms., ports., bibliography.

E184 .S23 O43 1967b

 Four thousand names arranged chronologically in the body of the book, but listed alphabetically in the index at the back for easy identification. Names are on left-hand pages, with date of arrival, ship's name, passenger's age, sex, and trade. Each right-hand page provides additional facts that

the authors have found in many other sources, such as birthplace and date, family affiliations, past activities in Sweden, e.g., military service, and all such facts are documented with references to sources consulted. For a continuation of passenger arrivals from 1851 through 1863, see Lagevik above.
   68088003

Rabe, Monica. *Kulturella glasögon: med svensk syn utomlands.* Göteborg: Tre böcker, [1992]. 81 p. Ill.

DL639 .R3 1992

A guide for the businessman or businesswoman who will travel abroad and work with foreigners. Interesting in the context of migration because it describes the Swedish way of viewing problems, solving them, and compares this with what the Swede may encounter abroad. Covers all aspects of living, including dress, ethical and moral problems, poverty, drugs, drinking, social life, nationalism, and everything that may be different from the Swedish norm.
   93161810

Ruff, Paul Miller. *Immanuel Lutheran Church, Irwin, Westmoreland County, parish records.* Greensburg, Pa.: P.M. Ruff, 1996. 148 p.

F159 .I78 R84 1996

   00301359

Simon, Bernice Hammar, ed. *The early history and church register record and ministerial accounts of the Swedish Mission Church of Youngstown, Ohio, 1886-1930: now, First Covenant Church of Youngstown, Ohio.* Canfield, OH (625 Blueberry Hill Dr., Canfield 44406): B.H. Simon, 1986. xiii, 127 p. Ill.

F499 .Y8 S56 1986

   86195580

Swedish Lutheran Church (Raccoon, N.J.). *The records of the Swedish Lutheran churches at Raccoon and Penns Neck, 1713-1786.* Translated and compiled by the Federal Writers' Project of the Works Progress Administration, State of New Jersey; with an introduction and notes by Dr. Amandus Johson. [Elizabeth, N.J.: Colby and McGowan, Inc.], 1938. xv, 387 p. Front. (facsims.), bibliography, indexes.

BX8076 .R27 S8

   39024680

Wright, F. Edward, comp. *Early church records of New Castle County. Holy Trinity Church (Wilmington, Del.). Records of Holy Trinity (Old Swedes) Church, Wilmington, Del., from 1697-1773.* 2 vols. Westminster, Md.: Family Line Publications, 1994. Map. Contents: vol. 1. [No special title]. vol. 2. *The records of Holy Trinity (Old Swedes) Church, Wilmington, Del., 1713-1799.* Translated from the original Swedish by Horace Burr, with an abstract of the English records. Bibliography, indexes.
Note: "Volume two is a reprint of the register of Old Swedes Church, taken from the translation by

Horace Burr, published by Historical Society of Delaware in 1890, entitled, 'The records of Holy Trinity (Old Swedes) Church.' "

F172 .N5 W75 1994

95138329

## IV. HANDBOOKS ON METHODOLOGY OF SWEDISH AND SWEDISH AMERICAN GENEALOGICAL RESEARCH

Almquist, Johan Ax[el]. *Svensk genealogisk litteratur*. 78 p.

Z5313 .S8 A5

A list of 455 works on genealogy, most of them family histories, known to the author. Bibliographical information is given, but almost no additional annotation. An index lists individuals and families included. Some of these books may be among the Library of Congress' holdings, but most are not. Some are undoubtedly in other libraries in the United States and Canada and can be located through online union catalogues. As of this writing (2002) the book is in very poor condition, with loose, yellowing pages that are flaking at the edges. The researcher who comes to the Library of Congress after this writing might check the Library's online catalogue to determine whether the book has been put on microfilm for preservation.

06008042

Brenner, S. Otto. *Personhistoriska källor för Skåne, Halland och Blekinge*. Reprotryk. [Lyngby]: Dansk Historisk Håndbogsforlag, 1977. 88 p.

CS921 .B7 1977

Overview of holdings of libraries, archives, and government offices that have records of vital statistics for Skåne, Halland, and Blekinge. Tells types of records and years covered and can save the researcher much time. Contents include Lansarkivet i Lund, Stadsarkivet i Malmö, Kulturen i Lund, Nordiska Museet i Stockholm, Det. kgl. Bibliotek i Köpenhamn, Kungl. Krigsarkivet i Stockholm, Lantmäterikontoren och Kungl. Lantmäteristyrelsen, Universitetsbiblioteket i Uppsala, Kungl. Biblioteket i Stockholm, Kungl. Statistiska Centralbyrån in Stockholm, Varbergs Museum, Skånska Konstmuseum i Lund, H.M. Kongens Håndbibliotek i Köpenhamn, Genealogiska Föreningen i Stockholm, Skånes Heraldiska Sällskap, Malmö, Blekinge Musei och Hembygdsförening i Karlskrona, Fleninge Släkt- och Bygde förening, Privatarkiv (enskilda arkiv), Skånes Genealogiska Förening, Statliga och kommunala svenska arkiv, Nordisk periodisk, genealogisk och heraldisk litteratur samt de nordiska föreningarna, Större utländska genealogiska tidskrifter, Större utländska genealogiska föreningar, Av intresse för forskningar i danska arkiv, Förteckning över kyrkoarkivalier i Landsarkivet i Lund, Förteckning över kyrkoarkivalier och mantalslängder i Stadsarkivet i Malmö.

78383532

Carlberg, Nancy Ellen. *Beginning Swedish research*. Anaheim, CA (1782 Beacon Ave. Anaheim, 92804-4515): Carlberg Press, 1989. 150, [9] leaves. Ill.

CS923 .C37 1989

Nineteen pages on Swedish names and genealogical charts. Three pages on Swedish calendar

differences and moveable feast days. Ten pages on the alphabet and a glossary of common words found in vital records. Twenty-one pages on sources of records in the United States. Twelve pages on sources for finding places in Sweden and glossaries of terms that occur in such sources. Sixty pages of explanations of the kinds of records that exist for Swedish research, many photocopies of actual records, how to read them, what information they contain and how to arrange the information in your own notes. The last eight pages list archives in the United States and Sweden, advice on doing research in Sweden, and a list of things to pack if you are going to Sweden.
  89156347

Clemensson, Per, and Kjell Andersson. *Släktforska!: steg för steg*. 4. rev. uppl. [4th rev. ed.] Stockholm: LT, 1993 [i.e., 1994]. 153 p. Ill., bibliography by subjects, index.
CS922 .C56 1993 Sweden

For the researcher who will be working with original records or with microform copies of them, this is a superb explanation of each kind of Swedish record that is useful to the genealogical researcher. The authors treat each kind of record separately, explain its origin and use, then give photocopies of actual records with sections of interest circled in red and arrows that lead from the circles to paragraphs that explain the significance of the material and any difficulties that may be associated with it, such as variant spellings, period handwriting, or abbreviations. Years covered by each kind of record are indicated. Pages 130-31 list handwritten variations of letters (as many as six or seven different shapes for some letters) for the seventeenth, eighteenth, and nineteenth centuries. Page 122 explains commonly used numbering systems for indicating generations in published family histories: Kekule von Strodonitz system, Rollers system, Hagers system, Lorenz system, and Engströms system. Glossary of common Latin words found in church records, page 132. Glossary of archaic medical terminology, page 133.
  94160815

Colling, Joyce, comp. *Swedish family research*. Burbank, CA (P.O. Box 4377, Burbank 91503): Southern California Genealogical Society, [1989]. 6 p., [1] leaf of plates. Ill., map.
CS922 .C65 1989

An overview for the beginner showing what records to look for and where to find them, first in the United States, then in Sweden. Appropriate repositories, with addresses, in both countries, and a good list of five books useful to the researcher. A one-page list of Swedish genealogical terms and a map of Sweden.
  89192500

Erickson, James E. (James Eldred), and Nils William Olsson. *Tracing your Swedish ancestry*. [New ed.]. New York: Swedish Information Service, 2000. 40 p. Ill.
CS922 .E75 2000

Presents the basic methodology for Swedish Americans who wish to research their family history beginning in America and working back to Sweden. Tells what documents to look for and where to find them. Lists societies, libraries, archives, and books in both America and Sweden.
  00705382

*Guide to Swedish-American archival and manuscript sources in the United States.* Chicago, Ill.: Swedish-American Historical Society, 1983. xxx, 600 p. Index.

Z1361 .S9G85 1983

Begins with a user's guide and the mailing addresses of repositories listed in the book. Each item is well annotated. Divided by state then by city, it reveals the existence of church records, membership lists of long-forgotten ethnic societies, interviews of individuals, and other records that a researcher could spend a lifetime without finding. The thirty-seven-page index lists authors, organizations, archives, places, individuals, and families and provides subject access to the main body of the book.

83050968

*Historical background affecting genealogical research in Sweden.* The Genealogical Department of the Church of Jesus Christ of Latter-day Saints. Rev. Salt Lake City, Utah, USA: The Department, 1976. 15 p. Ill., maps.

CS923 .H57 1976

82239274

Johansson, Carl Erik. *Cradled in Sweden.* Logan, Utah: Everton Publishers, 1972, 1977. 205 p. Ill., bibliography for each chapter.

CS922 .J6 1972

At present this may be the most nearly complete handbook in English for Americans who wish to research their Swedish forbears. A chapter on language gives good indications for pronunciation of Swedish. The description of the country includes explanations of ecclesiastical jurisdictions, records available, times and geographical areas covered by records; civil jurisdictions and their records are described. A map shows locations of jurisdictions named, lists of provinces with their component counties, and the designations of people from each province. Origin and formation of place names are explained, abbreviations for places listed, gazetteers and other sources indicated. Personal names are explained in detail and lists given of names that are for males, names for females, and names that are both. Because soldiers often took new
surnames when entering the military (to avoid a regiment with twenty Lindstroms, etc.), common "army and navy surnames" are listed. Special explanations are provided for names of tradesmen, the four most common ways of naming illegitimate children, names of emigrants, special cases, and a list of the nineteen most common surnames in Sweden from the most to the least common. There is an exhaustive list of Swedish archives and libraries. Special difficulties are addressed, such as fixed and movable feast days, calendar changes in Sweden, and the many different forms of handwriting. Pages 59-117 describe records available on film through the [Mormon] Library in Salt Lake City. On this point it is good to remember that the book was published in 1972 and is undoubtedly out of date. More records will be available now, and the Swedish SVAR project has made hundreds of thousands of records available through the Swenson Center at Augustana College in Rock Island, Illinois.

The book ends with lists of Swedish and Finnish army units and records available for them, companies and squadrons of Swedish army units and the regiments to which they belonged, a similar list in regimental order, probate records by county indicating years covered for each county,

a twenty-eight-page alphabetical list of all parishes in Sweden giving the name of the parish before and after 1952 and years for which records exist, a list of Swedish and Latin words commonly found in documents, and a brief bibliography by chapter.
79121364

Johansson, Egil. *Kyrkböckerna berättar*. Stockholm: LiberFörlag, 1983. 27 p. Ill.

DL991 .T853 J628 1983

Shows step by step how church records can be used not only for genealogical purposes, but also to reconstruct the entire daily life of a family or a community. Twenty-seven chapters illustrate the minutiae of the lives of Gertrud Ersdotter, her family, and her community in the village of Lilldelje in the parish of Tuna around the year 1820.
84125353

Lagerkranz, Gunnar. *Svenska sjukdomsnamn i gångna tider*. 3. uppl. [3$^{rd}$ ed.]. Göteborg: Sveriges släktforskarförbund, 1988. 143 p.

R121 .L18 1988

Diagnosed cause of death in documents varied as medical terminology evolved. This historical dictionary of names of diseases helps to decipher old records.
92138414

Lext, Gösta. *Studier i svensk kyrkobokföring 1600-1946*. Göteborg: Landsarkivet i Göteborg, 1984, 1985 printing. 383 p. Ill.

HA39 .S85 L49 1984

History of church records in Europe, but primarily in Sweden. This book will be of little use to the researcher seeking his or her Swedish roots and is not meant for this purpose; but for the researcher who wishes to be certified as a professional genealogical researcher for Sweden it will be of enormous help. It tells when records began, what laws required them, what information was required, and how information was set down before the state church was charged with this task.
88175716

*Over Øresund: en vejlednng for slægtsforskere*. [hovedredaktør, Steen Ousager.] København: ARKI. Varia, 1993. 60, 74 p. Ill.

CS903 .O94 1993

A bilingual book, the Swedish title is "Över Öresund, en handledning för släktforskare." The book's purpose is to help researchers whose ancestors emigrated the short distance to or from Denmark.
93217425

Pladsen, Phyllis J., and Joseph C. Huber, comp. *Swedish genealogical dictionary*. 2nd ed. White Bear Lake, MN (2185 Randy Ave., White Bear Lake 55110): Pladsen/Huber Press, 1993. v, 130 p. Ill.

CS6 .P55 1993

Approximately 1,500 words found in Swedish documents, with abbreviations when appropriate,

and English translations. Fifteen pages of handwriting samples with printed version of each that show varieties and peculiarities of script that researchers will encounter.
93224611

Saarinen, Jouni. *Roots in Sweden: the genealogist's guide to the Swedish archives*. [photographs, Kurt Eriksson; editing, Kerstin Abukhanfusa]. [Stockholm]: Riksarkivet, [1997]. 47 p. Ill., 1 map.

CS922 .S33 1997

What archives are there in Sweden and what do they contain? How does the researcher gain access to the material? What does the researcher do with them? The book addresses these questions. It explains what most Americans do not know: that when a person changed residence, he or she had to fill out a "flyttningslängd," a change of residence certificate; that these were registered in the "husförhörslängd," a catechetical register. There were lists of missing persons, passport lists, emigration lists, parish records, military and tax records, and records of sorts that Americans have never had to deal with. They are explained here. Page seventeen begins the chapter on "Where to find the records." Pages twenty-two and twenty-three contain a bibliography by categories: Genealogy in general, From the Swedish archives institutions, Registers of Swedish parishes, districts, etc., Dictionaries (this lists one genealogical dictionary), Swedish history in English, Registers in book form of Swedish emigrants, Aids to reading old handwriting, Addresses (lists annual publications that give addresses of administrative agencies). A map shows the provinces of Sweden. Pages twenty-six through forty-seven use the previous material to show how Tekla Lovisa Enlund, a 19th-century immigrant to America, used records, photocopies of which appear in the book, to trace her family. The authors carefully explain each step, and by the end of the book the reader has an excellent idea of what records there are, where to find them, and how to use them.
98128547

Sandström, Raija. *Finska och icke-finska tillnamn i Nedertorneås kyrkböcker på 1800-talet*. Umeå: Distribution, Institutionen för nordiska språk, Umeå universitet, 1985. xviii, 226 p.

CS2609 .N43 S26 1985

This doctoral dissertation may be of use to researchers whose ancestors came from Nedertorneå parish or the town of Haparanda and who may have been of Finnish descent.
85223027

*Swedish genealogical resources*. St. Paul, MN: Swedish Genealogy Group, Minnesota Historical Society, 1987, 1990 printing. 40 p.

E184 .S23 S945 1987

96118632

Swenson Swedish Immigration Research Center. *Swedish-American newspapers: a guide to the microfilms held by Swenson Swedish Immigration Research Center, Augustana College, Rock Island, Illinois*. Compiled by Lilly Setterdahl. Rock Island, Ill.: Augustana College Library, 1981. 36 p.

Z6953.5 .S9 S95 1981

81068299

Thomsen, Finn A. *The beginner's guide to Swedish genealogical research*. Bountiful, Utah: Thomsen's Genealogical Center, 1984. 23 p. Ill.
CS922 .T48 1984

An overview of Swedish names, kinds of documents one will need to consult and where to find them, the gothic alphabet, maps of the provinces and counties of Sweden, useful printed sources, and a relationship chart.
88148008

Thorsell, Elisabeth, i samverkan med Ulf Schenkmanis. *Släktforskning: vägen till din egen historia.* Västerås: ICA, 1993. 159 p. Ill.

CS922 .T49 1993

A thorough and lavishly illustrated textbook for genealogical research in Sweden, with occasional information on how to trace emigrants who went to America. Gives advice on interviewing family members, finding family mementos, and putting information together to create charts of relationships. Lists archives and describes their contents and uses: this chapter even gives advice for behavior in archives, such as maintaining silence in the reading rooms and reading the rules before using the institution. The many kinds of records are described, with the information they contain and problems that they can present. A unique feature of this book is the
 frequent insets that give invaluable tips that this compiler has not seen in other handbooks. For instance, in the chapter on church records the reader is reminded that a knowledge of Swedish history will prevent many otherwise insoluble problems; if one is researching a soldier who inexplicably disappears from church records around 1788, it may be because Sweden fought a war with Russia at that time.

Another inset explains terms used in old military records that indicate whether a soldier was absent from muster, or whether he (or his horse) were deemed suitable at muster. The book explains the SVAR project that is microfilming records at Ramsele (these are available in America through the Swenson Center at Augustana College in Rock Island, Illinois). Bibliographies are presented at the end for each chapter.
94200287

Warnstedt, Christopher von. *Krigsarkivet och släktforskaren: handledning och kommentarer.* [Stockholm]: Storstockholms genealogiska förening, [1989]. 48 p.

CS923 .W37 1989

A handbook for researching military records in the Krigsarkivet.
92138465

## V. LOCAL HISTORIES IN THE UNITED STATES

**California**
Beijbom, Ulf. *Guldfeber: en bok om guldrusherna till Kalifornien och Klondike.* Stockholm: Natur o. kultur, 1979. 223, [1] p. Ill., bibliography, index.

F1095 .K5 B44

Vivid description of gold rush fever as it affected people in Sweden and induced many to travel to

California or to the Klondike to make their fortunes. Filled with authentic drawings and photographs, the book describes advertising in Sweden, routes followed to reach California and Seattle, conditions during travel and after arrival, gold camps, techniques used to find gold, illustrates implements as simple as shovels and techniques as complex as transferring horses in slings from boats to dry land. Many Swedish pioneers are mentioned, but this is primarily a history of gold fever rather than a source for genealogical research.
  80460666

Skarstedt, Ernst Teofil.
*California och dess svenska befolkning.* Seattle, Wash., Tryckt hos Washington Printing Co., 1910. 463 p. incl. front. (port.) illus. fold. col. map.
  Med en färglagd karta öfver California, öfver 200 porträtt och 100 andra illustrationer. På eget förlg
. . . .
F870 .S23 S4

Information for immigrants and potential immigrants. The first 178 pages describe California city by city with detailed analysis of each region's possibilities for agriculture or industry. Chapters include history of the state up to 1846 (California soon after became part of the United States), history from 1845 to the time of publication (1910), topography, geography, rivers, valleys, lakes, and forests, a separate chapter on Death Valley and Yosemite Park, hunting, fishing, farming, the Indian, Chinese, and Japanese population; forty pages describe the principle cities. Detailed information on Swedish Lutheran, Methodist, Mission, and Baptist churches and congregations, Swedish newspapers in the state, and Swedish organizations. Pages 243-63 comprise a biographical dictionary of Swedes in California, with photographs of most and articles varying from one half to two pages. Many articles include photographs of families, houses, and places of business. Information in the articles emphasizes place of birth and family, date of emigration, date of arrival in America, date of arrival in California, and place[s] of residence in that state, with exhaustive histories of work and business for each individual, religious affiliation, and educational background. Includes color fold-out of Hammond's Map of California (copyright 1908) showing counties in different colors with all communities and topographical features.
  a 25000229

**Idaho**
Holmes, Alvin C. *Swedish homesteaders in Idaho on the Minidoka Irrigation Project, Minidoka County, Idaho.* [s.l.: s.n.], 1976 (Twin Falls: Ace Print.). 7, 120, [18] p. Ill.
F752 .M5 H64

The memoirs of the author from his parents' stories of their early life in Finland and in America, augmented by articles from the "Svenska amerikanaren tribunen" and aided by others, many still living at the time of publication. Covers the period 1892, when Isaac Erik Holmes emigrated from Finland to America, to 1972 when his wife Charlotta, "the last of the homesteaders in Big Bend" [p. 120] died. Appendix One gives a brief genealogy of the Holmes family; other appendices list members of societies and give newspaper clippings of local events. No index, but much information in the body of the text and many photographs of people, groups, buildings, and landscapes.
  77376021

**Illinois**

Johnson, Niel M., and Lilly Setterdahl. *Rockford Swedes: American stories*. Introduction by Ulf Beijbom; [based on] interviews by Lennart Setterdahl. East Moline, Ill.: American Friends of the Emigrant Institute of Sweden, 1993. vi, 372 p. Ill.

F549 .R7 J64 1993

The story of the evolution of Rockford, Illinois, as shown in interviews with fifteen Swedish immigrants and ten children of immigrants. Immigrants interviewed are Eric Ekebom, Helga Westerlind, Hjerdis Gustafson, Reuben Aldeen, Steven Northsea, Eric Carlson, Carl Linde, Hulda Linde, Martin Ostrom, Ruth Ostrom, Edwin Anderson, Karin Anderson, Anna Johnson, Venora Jernberg, and Gotthard Nilsson. Second generation interviewees are Richard Shelain, Mildred Lundell, Robert Brolin, David Broman, Burdette Carlson, Lawrence Gustafson, Roy Fridh, Arthur W. Anderson, and Irene and Eoy Hallstron. Earliest Rockford is fleshed out in the forty pages preceding the interviews with articles on early immigration, the first ethnic organizations, Rockford industry, Swedish ethnicity in East Rockford, the Swedish American press and temperance societies, socialist and singing societies, fraternal orders, and Swedish American landmarks. There are photographs of most persons interviewed.
93070085

Nordahl, Per. *Weaving the ethnic fabric: social networks among Swedish-American radicals in Chicago, 1890-1940*. Stockholm Almqvist & Wiksell International, 1994. xvi, 245 p., [1] folded leaf of plates: ill., maps.

F548.9.S23 N67 1994

The author's dissertation, written at Umeå University. Describes how three Swedish working-class organizations cooperated to promote their interests in an American environment. In so doing, they used a form of "folkrörelsesamverkan," (popular movement cooperation) fashioned after techniques known to them in Sweden. They were so successful that by the 1930s Swedish Americans were fully integrated into the American labor movement.
95130413

Nyblom, Gösta, ed. *Americans of Swedish descent; how they live and work*. Rock Island, Ill., G. Nyblom Pub. House [1948]. 600 p. Ills., ports.

E184 .S23 N9

History of Swedish life in Illinois, based on more than a thousand biographies of people from all walks of life. Chapter titles of the first part are "The story of the immigrants as revealed in their letters" by Dr. O. N. Olson, "The immigrant and religion" by Dr. C. G. Carlfelt, "Swedish American educational enterprises" by Dr. Conrad Bergendoff, "The immigrants and their descendants in American politics" by Dr. Fritiof Ander, "The fine arts among Swedish Americans in Illinois " by D. E. E. Ryden, "Swedish non-sectarian organizations" by Carl Stockenberg, "The older settlements" by Dr. Ernst W. Olson, "The Swedes in Moline" by Emil Swanson, "The Swedes in Rockford" by Herman G. Nelson, "The Swedes in Chicago" by Alida Bergquist, and "The Swedish club of Chicago" by Herbert R. Hedman. Many individuals are mentioned, with background in Sweden and salient biographical information.

The second part contains seventeen pages of articles on life in Sweden. The third part (pp. 319-600)

is an alphabetical listing of biographies. These entries are two to five paragraphs long and contain data on birth, immigration, and family when appropriate. All parts are copiously illustrated with photographs of people, groups, landscapes, and buildings.
   49013181

Olson, Ernst Wilhelm, ed., in collaboration with Anders Schön and Martin J. Engberg. *History of the Swedes of Illinois.* 2 vols. 1908. Reprint. New York: Arno Press, 1979. Ill.

F550 .S8 O5 1979

  An encyclopedic work on the subject up to the date of publication, 1908. Naming names, places, and dates, the first volume (933 pages) devotes chapters to detailed histories of the state of Illinois, the city of Chicago, the first Swedes in Illinois, the Bishop Hill Colony and other early settlements, the Swedish Methodist-Episcopal Church, the Swedish Episcopal Church, the Swedish Lutheran Church, the Swedish Baptist Church, the Swedish Mission Church, Swedes in the Civil War, Music and musicians, Press and literature, Art and artists, and Swedish organizations. Two-page bibliography and twelve-page index. Most pages contain at least one photograph or drawing of persons, groups, houses, or businesses. Divisions within chapters of the first volume are by place or person, depending on their importance; some sections amount to histories of particular counties, some to biographies, some to histories of church buildings, but always with names and dates that place them within the framework of the history of Swedes in Illinois. Volume two consists of two parts: Biographical sketches of Swedes of Chicago, 416 pages including an eleven-page name index, with an average of two biographies per page. This provides a photograph of each person and information on birth, immigration, family antecedents, current family, education, extensive information on professional background, membership in ethnic organizations, education, publications, and achievements. Almost no women are included as main entries, but they can be found under articles on fathers, brothers, or husbands. Part three, still in volume two, 268 pages including a three-page index, lists biographical sketches of "counties at large," i.e., not Chicago. This is arranged by town or county, with persons appearing alphabetically in each section. Information provided is of the same kind as in part two, but significantly more women appear as main entries.
   78015844

O'Neill, Linda. *History, memory, and ethnic identification: rediscovering community in Bishop Hill, Illinois.* DeKalb, Ill.: LEPS Press, 1996. xiv, 145 p. Bibliography.

F549 .B6O54 1996

  Bishop Hill was a community founded in 1846 by Eric Jansson and his followers, who dissented from the formalism of the Swedish state church. That church had forbidden Jansson to perform services in its name, and he and others from Hälsingland made the journey to the American heartland. By 1861 the exclusively religious nature of the community had dissolved, but much later, when the dialect of Hälsingland had disappeared in Sweden, linguists found it still being spoken in Bishop Hill. The town suffered many severe blows, including the murder of Jansson; a visit of some notables to a Shaker community and their subsequent ban on marriage drove many people to settle in other towns, and the community dwindled until in the 1940s fewer than two hundred people lived there. Nonetheless, Bishop Hill, its history, its historical crafts, have caused an increased desire in some Swedish Americans to connect with their past, and the town has become a focal point for several

organizations that wish to do this. This book is a result of interviews with people who live in Bishop Hill. Three-page chronology of events in Bishop Hill 1808-1996.
  6021680

*The Swedes in Knox County, Illinois: a translation into English of portions of Eric Johnson and C.F. Peterson's Svenskarne i Illinois (Swedes in Illinois)*. Leroy Williamson, trans. Edited and published by the Knox County Genealogical Society. Galesburg, Ill.: The Society, 1979. Swedish title: *Svenskarne i Illinois*. 71 p.

F547 .K7 J6413 1979

  A history of Knox County emphasizing genealogical information. Eight-page index of personal names. Entries for persons give information on birth and family background, profession, religious affiliation, and marriage. Lists of Swedish organizations in each town, Swedish employees in businesses, Swedish owners of businesses, Swedish elected officials, Swedish churches, and Civil War roll of the Swedish Company in the Illinois 43rd Regiment.
  81184486

Williamson, Leroy. *The Swedes in Knox County, Illinois: a translation into English of portions of Eric Johnson and C.F. Peterson's Svenskarne i Illinois (Swedes in Illinois)*. Edited and published by the Knox County Genealogical Society. Galesburg, Ill.: The Society, 1979. 71 p.

F547 .K7 J6413 1979

  A history of Knox County emphasizing genealogical information. Eight-page index of personal names. Entries for persons give information on birth and family background, profession, religious affiliation and marriage. Lists of Swedish organizations in each town, Swedish employees in businesses, Swedish owners of businesses, Swedish elected officials, Swedish churches, and Civil War roll of the Swedish Company in the Illinois 43rd Regiment.
  81184486

**Iowa**
Swan, Gustaf N. (Gustaf Nelson). *Svenskarna i Sioux City: några blad ur deras historia*. Chicago: Jacobson Printing Co., 1912. 262 p. Ill.

F629 .S6 S97

  An encyclopedic history of Swedes in Sioux City up to 1912. Lists ethnic organizations, newspapers, and magazines, Swedish Americans active in local business and politics, religion, and in this case Sioux City as the site of a Swedish consulate. It even lists Swedish books in the public library. Under each subject, members or prominent people are named, and the last chapter, pages 236-53, provides brief biographies of those who were the first settlers, "de som voro med från början." The single illustration is a photograph of the author in his study. No index.
  14002491

**Kansas**
Bergin, Alfred. *Lindsborg: bidrag till svenskarnas och den Lutherska kyrkans historia i Smoky Hill River dalen: samlade påuppdrag af Bethania-församlingen i Lindsborg, Kansas, för fyrtio-års-festen af Alfred Bergin*. Lindsborg: Bethania-församlingen, 1909. 368 p. Ills., map.

F689 .L7 B4

Doctor Bergin wrote his history of the town forty years after the first settlers arrived and was able to interview many who had been there from the beginning. More than four hundred photographs illustrate the almost day-by-day history, naming nearly everyone who resided in the community and its environs. No index. The final fourteen pages are advertisements for businesses. Ruth Billdt's *Pioneer Swedish-American culture in central Kansas*, listed in the present bibliography, is a translation of this book, with the photographs, but without the advertisements.
09014464

Bergin, Alfred. *Lindsborg efter femtio år; bidrag till vår lutherska kyrkas och svenskarnas historia i Kansas och Sydvästern*. Lindborg, Bethania-församlingen [1919]. 239 p. Ills., ports.

F689 .L7 B42

Written ten years after Bergin's first history of the town, this book studies all aspects of life in Lindsborg, with long lists of members of societies, and emphasizes the town's deep religiosity and its relationship to Bethany College. Ruth Billdt's *The Smoky valley in the after years* is a translation of this book.
19011607

Bergin, Alfred. *Pioneer Swedish-American Culture in Central Kansas*. Translated by Ruth Billdt. Lindsborg, Kan.: Lindsborg News-Record, printers, 1965. 163, 92 p. Ill., maps (on lining papers), ports.

F689 .L7 B413 1965

Translation of *Lindsborg, bidrag till svenskarnas och den lutherska kyrkans historia i Smoky Hill River dalen*. The inside back cover provides a two-page street map of Lindsborg on a scale of 600 feet to an inch.
71020083

Billdt, Ruth Bergin, and Elizabeth Jaderborg, eds. *The Smoky Valley in the after years*. Lindsborg, Kan.: Lindsborg News-Record, 1969. 220, vii p. Ill., map, ports., index.

F689 .L7 B54

Translation of Alfred Billdt's "Lindsborg efter femtio år." This book includes an eighty-seven page "Part Two--from the files," apparently by the translator, with a wealth of drawings and fascinating photographs of Lindsborg folk through the years, biographies, and odd pieces of information. Part Two has its own bibliography of sources consulted and even some corrections to the original book. The researcher who is interested in the original should also consult the translation for these additions.
78023293

Lindquist, Emory Kempton. *Smoky Valley people: a history of Lindsborg, Kansas*. Lindsborg, Kan.: Bethany College, 1953. x, 269 p. [15] p. of plates, ills., bibliography.

F689 .L7 L5

A history of the town based on the belief that Lindsborg and Bethany College possess values that cannot easily be duplicated elsewhere. Knowing this as the starting point, the reader can enjoy extremely detailed histories of movements and organizations that culminated in the Smoky Valley

town of 1953. These histories include long lists of participants in movements, members of societies, contributors to worthy causes, settlers, and businessmen, not many of whom are found in the sparse three-page index at the end. Chapters treat the arrival of the Swedes in Smoky Valley, the founding of their church, how the people lived, founding and development of Bethany College, the Bethany College Oratorio Society's performance of Handel"s "The Messiah" annually on Palm and Easter Sunday and Bach's "The Passion of Our Lord According to Saint Matthew" on Good Friday, a chapter on Dr. Carl Swensson, a description of a stroll along Main Street with points of interest that recur in Swedish American literature: Swedish churches and Swedish-owned businesses. Chapters follow on "the Swedish element," churches, schools and civic life, artists and writers, and the activities and future of Bethany College. Twenty-four photographs, of which eleven portray individuals or the singing societies of the college, and the rest portray old Swedish homesteads, college buildings, and two interesting pictures of Main Street in 1878 and again in 1953. An excellently selected, eight-page bibliography includes sections on manuscripts, newspapers, biography, Bethany College, and the college's "Messiah."
53013457

Runwall, Anders, and Bertil Hagert. *Lindsborg--svenskstaden i USA:s mitt.* Vällingby: Harrier, 1979. 78 p. Ill., maps.

F689 .L7 R86

Excellent color and black and white photographs show old and contemporary (i.e., as of 1979) Lindsborg. The text gives basic history and facts. Map of Saline County, and a street map of Lindsborg.
79368399

Wheeler, Wayne. *An analysis of social change in a Swedish-immigrant community: the case of Lindsborg, Kansas.* New York: AMS Press, 1986. 386 p. Ill., statistical tables, bibliography, maps, index.

F689 .L7 W48 1986

"The instance of Lindsborg, Kansas, is presented to indicate how continuity and cultural themes can be used to examine social change," (page 1 of Introduction). This the author's stated aim, and the book is a scholarly but highly readable history of the evolution of Swedish ethnicity in this particularly important part of Swedish America. Chapters treat the old-world background, new-world settlement, the family, the frontier and youth culture, educational institutions, religion, a fascinating thirty-page chapter on pioneers, heroes, and rituals, and ends with the influence of the outside [American] world.
83045362

**Maine**
Klein, Barbro Sklute. *Legends and folk beliefs in a Swedish American community.* 2 vols. New York: Arno Press, 1980. Maps, bibliography.

GR111 .S84 K57 1980

A doctoral dissertation studying old-world folk beliefs as they evolved in the town of New Sweden, Maine. Legendary beings studied are the devil, trolls, näcken, skogsrå, tomten, spöken and the

"clever people." The study includes immigrants, their children, and their grandchildren, and the final chapter treats folk beliefs in relation to 1. "The accommodations, intrusions, and changes in lore localized in old Sweden," 2. "Transference into the American milieu of narrative models," 3. "Acceptance of new beliefs and new tale patterns from Yankees and Frenchmen," and 4. "The discarding of Old World beliefs and legends."
  80000730

## Minnesota

Dahl, Mildred Anderson, comp. *Spruce Hill remembered.* New Brighton, Minn.: The Author, 1996. 530 p. Ill.

F614 .S67 D34 1996

   Written from the viewpoint of the Anders Anderson family, this is truly an exhaustive history of Spruce Hill in general. The area covered is specifically "a parcel of ground surveyed as: Town 130N, Range36W, later known as Spruce Hill . . . ." [preface]. Using public and private records, the author has produced a tour de force that traces the history of Spruce Hill section of land by section of land, sometimes giving photographs of the same piece of ground in different time periods and pointing out changes in landscape or additions of buildings. Most pages contain several photographs or drawings, many in color, with sections of plat maps, aerial photographs, and exact dimensions of lots. Private homes, businesses, churches, cemeteries are described with names of all people involved. A five-page bibliography of works cited provides additional sources for researchers. No index, but this is a work of genuine scholarship, and invaluable to anyone having a connection to Spruce Hill.
  97140798

McKnight, Roger. *Moberg's emigrant novels and the Journals of Andrew Peterson: a study of influences and parallels.* New York: Arno Press, 1979. v, 235 p.

PT9875 .M5 Z835 1979

   See the next annotation (Mihelich) for the relevance of this entry.
  78015196

Mihelich, Josephine. *Andrew Peterson and the Scandia story: a historical account about a Minnesota pioneer whose diaries have been "reborn as a piece of world literature" through Vilhelm Moberg and his writings.* Minneapolis, MN.: Co-published by the author and Ford Johnson Graphics, 1984. viii, 202 p. [1] folded leaf of plates, ill., maps.

F614 .S53 M54 1984

   Andrew Peterson was a noted horticulturist and active in his community near the city of Waconia in Laketown Township. More important for today's researcher are the diaries he kept from 1855 to 1898 chronicling daily life, and the religious, social, and political events of his time and place. Unfortunately, he seldom mentioned individuals. Ms. Mihelich has written the present work to flesh out the world that Peterson took for granted and did not commit to paper. She has traced property owners and numbered them so that their holdings can be found on a fold-out map on page twenty. She provides information on individuals and families, with many photographs, a bibliography for each chapter, and a seven-page index containing primarily personal and place names. Peterson's diaries have additional importance because they formed the background that writer Vilhelm Moberg

(whose works are listed in the present bibliography) used for his four-volume epic of a Swedish family's travail during emigration to and settlement in America.
84080917

Porter, Robert B., ed. *A guide to the historical records of Chisago Lake Colony, Minnesota.* Center City, Minn.: R.B. Porter, 1982. 253 p. Ill.

F612 .C45 P67 1982

Chisago Lake Colony was populated almost exclusively by Swedish immigrants. It was isolated, and did not begin to keep some kinds of records until the late 1870s. This book attempts to present records dating from the beginning of the settlement up to the 1870s, although in many cases it goes up to the 1930s or the 1940s.
83147774

Porter, Robert B.
*The secrets of Glader: Minnesota's oldest Swedish cemetery.* Center City, Minn.: Ancestors, 1989. 229 p. Ill., bibliography for each chapter, index.

F614 .C35 P67 1989

History of the cemetery with much history of the Chisago settlement. Lists of persons buried in Glader Cemetery, many photographs of tombstones, of the surrounding landscapes, and of nineteenth-century documents including land sales, hotel registers, and even a grocery list.
89084040

Setterdahl, Lilly. *Minnesota Swedes.* 2 vols. [East Moline, Ill.]: American Friends of the Emigrant Institute of Sweden, 1996-1999. Ills., statistical tables, extensive bibliography.

F612 .G6 S48 1996

This book is based on the premise that it is particularly valuable to present a picture of the immigrant experience from beginning to end, or as stated by Robert C. Ostergren of the University of Wisconsin-Madison, "linked data covering all phases of the migration experience from the circumstances that led to emigration . . . to the adaptations necessary . . . in America," [Foreword]. For the purpose, the author describes the migration from Trolle Ljungby in Sweden to Goodhue County, Minnesota, during the years 1855 to 1912, the circumstances that caused people to leave their homes (the push) and the circumstances that caused them to choose Goodhue County as their destination (the pull). There are letters covering 1855-1881 to Bengt Anderson and from Swen Olson, Ola Anderson, Swea Andersson, Bengta Nilson, N. P. Granquist, and Ola Nilsson. It also includes a hundred pages of interviews with the following descendants: Bernard Anderson, Eldon Anderson, Arlan Banks, Betty Bender, Ole Brodd, Gladys Eckholm, Virginia Fanslow, Helen Fredrickson, Steven Hedeen, Myrtle Hilan, Helen Hyllengren, Stella Ingeman, Donald L. Johnson, Donley Lamberg, Doris Landon, Elsie Mae Lersch, Everal Nelson, Harriet Nelson, Lawrence Nelson, Norris Nelson, Sharon Nelson, Janet Larson, Sterling Nelson, Janice Olson, Mildred Peterson, Arnold, Risberg, Earl Skog, Aurora Swanson, Stanley Swanson, Walter Swanson, Milton Swenson, Marian Terborch, Loraine Dened, Marlene Thompson, Donald Trulen, Hazel Weberg, Wallace Weber, Betty Jane Withers, and Richard Young.
96085955

*Swedes in the Twin Cities  immigrant life and Minnesota's urban frontier*. Edited by Philip J. Anderson and Dag Blanck. St. Paul, Minn.: Minnesota Historical Society Press, 2001. x, 367 p. Ill., maps.

F614 .M6 S94 2001

Six articles under **Aspects of Urban Settlement**: 1. Immigrants and the Twin Cities: melting pot or mosaic?, by Rudolph J. Vecoli. Skillful debunking of myths concerning "our immigrant ancestors," and discussion of ethnicity. 2. Why Minnesota, Why the Twin Cities?, by M. Arnold Barton. Sets forth traditional explanations that Minnesota resembled the Swedish wooded country, then points out that only part of the state fits this description. In fact, Swedes flourished on the prairies of Kansas and Nebraska as well. Suggests that "timing, opportunity, transportation, and promotion" [p. 32] were also important. 3. Swedish neighborhoods of the Twin Cities, by David A. Lanegran. Describes ethnic diversity of the Twin Cities through the years. Maps of St. Paul and of Minneapolis showing numbers of Swedish-born residents in various neighborhoods in 1895, 1905, 1910, 1920, and 1930. 4. "Unfortunates" and "City Guests": Swedish American inmates and the Minneapolis City Workhouse, 1907, by Joy K. Lintelman. Studies inmates by age, offenses, occupation, marital status, seasonality of incarceration (all ethnic groups suffered less incarceration in summer, more in winter), has a separate section on women. Offered as a "beginning in researching the 'darker' side of Swedish immigrant life . . . . " [p. 74]. 5. Evelina Johansdotter, textile workers, and the Munsingwear family: class, gender, and ethnicity in the political economy of Minnesota at the end of World War I., by Lars Olsson. Immigrant women in the labor force. 6. The Northern neighbor, Winnipeg, the Swedish service station in the "Last Best West," 1890-1950, by Lars Ljungmark. Differences between Swedish settlers in the United States and in Canada.

Six articles under **Institutional and Creative Life**: 7. The Swedish Historical Society of America: the Minnesota years, by Byron J. Nordstrom. A study of this earliest of such societies, its demise, and the rise to prominence of other groups. 8. Swan Johan Turnblad and the Founding of the American Swedish Institute, by Nils William Olsson and Lawrence G. Hammerstrom. Brief biography of Turnblad and the beginning of the Institute. 9. Brothers whether dancing or dying: Minneapolis's Norden Society, 1871-198?, by William C. Beyer. The activities of a society that lasted more than a hundred years, and whose written records record the day-to-day concerns of its members. 10. Pictures from a new home: Minnesota's Swedish American artists, by Mary Towley Swanson. History of immigrants and first-generation American artists, including a few women, who show an amazing variety of vision. Covers mid-nineteenth century to the 1990s. Includes commentary on the social and financial concerns that helped or hindered. 11. Performing ethnicity: the role of Swedish theatre in the Twin Cities, by Anne-Charlotte Harvey. Studies Swedish-language theater as it evolved, and its effectiveness in promoting a feeling of Swedish ethnicity in the audiences. 12. Dania Hall: at the center of a Scandinavian American community, by David Markle. Nineteen pages chronicling the history of a building erected originally by Danes, but which became a pan-Scandinavian center of theater and social activity for more than a hundred years.

Four articles under **The Language of Immigrant Experience**: 13. Forskaren: a Swedish radical voice in Minneapolis, 1894-1924, by Michael Brook. History of a newspaper turned magazine that occasionally raised eyebrows and kept Scandinavians in touch with one another through letters to the editor. Gives brief biographies of some important figures of the time. 14. Svenska amerikanska

posten: an immigrant newspaper with American accents, by Ulf Jonas Björk. Points out that more than 225 Swedish-language newspapers were published in the United States to serve the more than one million immigrants from Sweden. The newspaper here discussed was published from 1885 to 1940, and this is the history of its evolution as the needs and character of its subscribers evolved and made it one measure of the development of Swedish America. 15. Teaching Swedish in the public schools: cultural persistence in Minneapolis, by Anita Olson Gustafson. A history of foreign-language curricula in the city's public schools. In 1905, Minneapolis had the second largest population of Swedes in America (after Chicago) with 38,000 people. Twenty-nine percent of the city's population was foreign-born. 16. American
Swedish revisited, by Nils and Patricia Hasselmo. A very brief history of the Swedish language in the United States. 17. Libraries, immigrants, and communities: perspectives on the Swedish immigrant experience in the Twin Cities 1889-1917, by Kermit B. Westerberg. Overview of professional literature among librarians on needs of multilingual and multicultural communities.

Five articles on **Swedes in Religion and Politics**: 18. As others saw them: Swedes and American religion in the Twin Cities, by Mark A. Granquist. Swedish immigrants formed new denominations, and in America they often borrowed elements from American denominations. Within the religious heterogeneity of the Twin Cities, this article discusses Swedish adaptations. 19. Ethnicity and religion in the Twin Cities: community identity through gospel music, and education, by Scott E. Erickson. A study of the revivalist work of Erik August Skogsbergh and of the Mission Covenant Church in helping immigrants to avoid dissolution in the American melting pot and to maintain their own sense of ethnic identity. 20. David F. Swenson, evolution, and public education in Minnesota, by Philip J. Anderson. Biography of Swenson, history of his
opposition to legislation that would have outlawed the teaching of the theory of evolution, descriptions of his championing of academic freedom through spirited exchanges with local newspapers. 21. Swedish Americans and the 1918 gubernatorial campaign in Minnesota, by Dag Blanck. Swedes formed 11.5 percent of the state's population and were its second largest immigrant group. Candidate Charles Lindbergh's isolationist platform represented rural opinion, while urban Swedish Americans tended to oppose it, as shown in Swan Turnblad's "Svenska amerikanska posten," and this election brought to light the evolving differences among groups within Swedish America. 22. Gubernatorial politics and Swedish Americans in Minnesota: the 1970 election and beyond, by Bruce L. Larson. In 1998 Jesse Ventura became one of the state's few non-Scandinavian governors. This article is a study of social and political forces at work since 1970.

All the articles, except article 16, are followed by extensive notes that serve both as explanatory and bibliographical aids.
00052543

**New Jersey**
Federal Writers' Project. *The Swedes and Finns in New Jersey . . . written and illustrated by the Federal Writers' Project of the Works Progress Administration, State of New Jersey; with an introd. by Amandus Johnson . . . sponsored by the New Jersey commission to commemorate the 300th anniversary of the settlement by the Swedes and Finns on the Delaware, D. Stewart Craven, chairman.* [Bayonne, N.J., Jersey Print. Co.], 1938. 6 p., l., 165 p. Front., plates, ports., bibliography, index.

F137 .F32

A guide book to, and history of, sites in New Jersey founded by Swedes and Finns. Most events described took place in the 17th and 18th centuries; information on the sites' present circumstances (as of the date of publication) is given primarily to aid the tourist in finding them. Chapters on the Swedish background, Where three nations met, Minuit founds New Sweden, The Swedes purchase New Jersey, Printz builds Fort Elfsborg, Sweden rules the Delaware, "Big Belly" vs. "Peg-Leg," The fall of New Sweden, Settlements on New Jersey creeks, The rise of the churches, English and German influences, A portrait of New Sweden, The second fall of New Sweden, The Swedes and Finns as Americans, Swedesboro, Penns Neck, The Glebe, Repaupo, Port Elizabeth, Friesburg Church, and Fort Elfsborg. Twenty-six drawings and photographs. A five-page chronology covering 1609 to 1938.
38025885

Turp, Ralph K. *West Jersey under four flags*. Philadelphia: Dorrance, 1975. vii, 305 p. Ill.
F145 .S8 T87

A "study of the socioeconomic factors experienced by the middle class people" [Introduction] during the period from 1638 to 1909. The largest part of the book covers the colonial and post-colonial period, with some nineteenth-century material, describing daily life in all aspects including slavery, employment, religion, and social life. Seventeen tables list members of the Mansson family, the Steelman family, families living in Old Gloucester County during the first half of the eighteenth century, land purchases of the Steelman family, colonial taverns of West Jersey, primary and secondary land purchases in Cape May County, the Jeremy Adams family, colonial governors of New Jersey, some individuals who served in the Revolution from Gloucester and Cape May Counties, ships calling at Batsto, Bog Iron Works (locations, builders, dates opened and closed), business statistics of Gloucester County in 1832, the 1794 militia enrollment of Gloucester County, births and deaths in the John Turp family, the William Steelman Foster family. Thirty-six drawings and photographs, mostly of buildings. Maps of Sweden, New Sweden, Colonial New Jersey, Tuckahoe, and sites of Revolutionary War skirmishes in West Jersey. Brief bibliographical notes after each chapter. Five-page bibliography. Index lists few individuals, but the text, if read in its entirety, mentions hundreds of names and relationships. The book can be of great use for the patient genealogist, and provides rich details for those wishing a picture of their ancestors' everyday lives or those who wish to write fiction set in this time and place.
76351173

**New York**
Moe, M. Lorimer, ed. and principal author. *Saga from the hills: a history of the Swedes of Jamestown, New York*. Jamestown, N.Y.: Fenton Historical Society, 1983. xxvii, 688 p. Ill., ports.
F129 .J3 M64 1983

Study of the Swedes of Jamestown, New York, from first settlement, naming almost all individuals involved. Presented in parts by subject: Why did Swedes settle in Jamestown? Public servants and the press, listing mayors, national and state office holders, other elected and appointed officials, policemen, firemen, and journalists. Swedes in the military and in aviation, including the Civil War, the Fenton Guards, the Spanish-American War, World Wars I and II, and the Korean and Vietnam

wars. Industry and business, including lumber mills, the furniture industry, financial institutions, and many families and individuals involved. Lists grocers, restaurateurs, bakers, tailors, haberdashers, and stores. Health professions, including dentists, nurses and pharmacists. Artists, musicians, actors, athletes. Thirty-two page description of Swedish organizations. Almost every page has black-and-white photographs of people, buildings, and parts of the city. Concludes with the following appendices: A view of the city (text only, no photographs), 1889, by A. J. Lannes (five pages), How our family name [Sundell] originated, by Gustaf Johanson Sundell (four pages), Chautauqua visit in 1892, by Mrs. Charles Jaderstrom (one page), Swedish American journalist, excerpts from O. W. Anderson's journal (one and one half pages), History of the First Lutheran Church of Jamestown, by Daniel L. Carlson (one page). Eight pages of lists as follows: Swedish American aldermen and councilmen since Jamestown became a city in 1887, Swedish American members of the Board of Education, Chautauqua County officials, Swedish Americans in principal appointive offices, World War I honor roll, Norden Club charter members and past presidents, baseball "oldtimers," Roger Tory Peterson, Jamestown's Swedish teachers.
7139256

Ödman, Per-Olof. *De sista svenskarna: om svenskamerikaner i Brooklyn, New York*. Helsinborg: Fyra förläggare, [1976]. [112] p. Ill.

F128.9 .S23 O34

An intimate history of some Swedish immigrants and many Americans of Swedish descent resident in Brooklyn. Lavishly illustrated with black and white photographs of people and of street scenes with substantive text that gives a well-rounded idea of Swedish American life in Brooklyn. Hundreds of names, birthplaces, dates, and family relationships are given in the text, but there is no index for fast location.
78344856

### South Dakota
Dahl, K. G. Wm. (K.G. William Dahl). *Children of the prairie*. Translated from the Swedish by Emeroy Johnson. [Nebraska?]: S. Dahl and M.D. Lindgren. (Minden, NE: Fifth Street Print.), 1984. 48 p. Ill.

F660 .S23 D3413 1984

Sketches of pioneer life in South Dakota by a Swedish-born pastor who served several churches and ministered to both whites and Indians. Three pages of black and white photographs including four photographs of Indians on a reservation, and one of the early main street of White Rock, South Dakota. Sketches are entitled "The gray horses," "The palefaces," "The bridge," "The homesteader's boy," "Christmas on the prairies," "Black Karin," and "Just a little gentian."
86218299

### Texas
Hellström, Tommy. *Pionjärerna från Värmland: de okända svenskarna på Texas prärie*. [Karlstad]: T. Hellström, [1996]. 127 p. Ill. (some col.), map, bibliography, index.

F395 .S23 H45 1996

The story of immigrants from Värmland, many of whom settled in Texas. Personal histories of

daily life and the building of businesses and homes, with all their attendant problems, difficulties, and failures. Good for the genealogist and for those seeking an idea of how people lived from the journey by ship to success or failure in the new country. Rich in illustrations, with an index of all persons mentioned and a brief bibliography.
   96225024

Scott, Larry E. (Larry Emil). *The Swedish Texans*. 1st ed. [San Antonio, Tex.]: University of Texas Institute of Texan Cultures at San Antonio, 1990. 288 p. Ill., partial index.
F395 .S23 S44 1989

   An engaging book that goes beyond a simple statistical listing of organizations and institutions. People are individuals with personalities that include admirable and sometimes unenviable traits, so that parts of the book read like a novel. The first one hundred pages describe Texas in the 1850s and the early Swedish settlers who chose to live there. With the Civil War, Swedish settlers had to consider slavery and politics, and the last 140 pages describe Swedish institutions, place names, language, press, writers, colleges, and cultural groups in Texas, as well as the Galveston flood and Swedes in the cities. Extensive bibliographical notes for each of the twenty chapters, and an eleven-page bibliography that includes manuscript sources and the Swante Palm papers in the Barker Texas History Center Archives in Austin. Black and white drawings and photographs of buildings, individuals, families, and documents. The index lists only a few of the names found in the text.
   89016656

Severin, Ernest. *Swedes in Texas in words and pictures, 1838-1918: English translation*. Translator, Christine Andreason; coordinating editor, James Christianson. [Swedish title: *Svenskarne i Texas i ord och bild, 1838-1918.*] [Austin, Tex.]: New Sweden 88 Austin Area Committee, 1994. xix, 1,209 p. Ill., map.
F395 .S23 S45 1994

   An exhaustive history of each subject discussed, with biographies and photographs of most persons named and photographs of buildings, families, and societies. Begins with history, geography and government of Texas. Continues with Swedish immigration and the foundation of churches, colleges, and societies, each one described in detail with names of persons involved and many photographs. Has sections on the following colonies, with many biographies for each: Austin, Palm Valley, Brushy, Georgetown, Taylor, Hutto, Decker, Ericsdale, Jonah, Elroy, Kenedy, Manor, East Sweden, West Sweden, Brady, Melvin, Fort Worth, El Campo, Dallas, Waco, Lund, Kimbro, Manda, Ganado, Crosby, Elgin, Louise, Galveston, Olivia, Temple, Swedonia, Bishop, Swensondale, Lyford, San Antonio, and Houston. Nineteen-page index of personal names. Formal style quite different from the lively presentation of Scott's book above, but with so much detailed information that the genealogist, the historian, and the novelist all may find it useful.
   94206344

**Wisconsin**
Hale, Frederick. *The Swedes in Wisconsin*. Madison: State Historical Society of Wisconsin, 1983. 32 p. Ill., ports.
F590 .S23 H34 1983

The story of six men and a dog who left Gävle in 1841 and ended up in Wisconsin to found a colony called Nya Uppsala. The leader of the group was the famous Gustaf Unonius. This brief introduction takes Swedish settlement of the state up to the 1920s and provides good basic information, including a one-page bibliography and five pages of black and white photographs.
  82023272

*Letters relating to Gustaf Unonius and the early Swedish settlers in Wisconsin.* Translated and edited by George M. Stephenson; assisted by Olga Wold Hansen. Rock Island, Ill.: Augustana Historical Society, 1937. 151 p.
F536 .A96 vol. 7

Of Finnish-Swedish descent, Unonius' work plays a major roll in the history of the great Swedish migration to North America. This volume, specifically about settlement in Wisconsin, presents a wide variety of subjects; most of the letters are neither by nor to Unonius, but all discuss subjects of great importance to the time and place. Some are letters to newspapers, others to family members or acquaintances. Many details of daily life for the population in general, not only for immigrants.
  39021164

## VI. PERSONAL NAMES

Allén, Sture, and Staffan Wåhlin. *Förnamnsboken.* Stockholm: AWE/Geber, 1979. 258 p.
CS2375 .S8 A55

A product of Göteborg University's Swedish name project, this book "is based on the complete names of the total population of Swedish citizens as recorded in the national registration files on January 1, 1973" [p. 17]. The names number 10,562, not taking into account names that are held by fewer that ten persons. They are first names only; and are listed alphabetically with the number of people bearing each name, the sex to which the name refers, the part of the country in which it is most common, the decades in which it has been most popular, and the ratio of its frequency in comparison to the other names in the list. Brief additional lists of the fifty most common names for men and for women, the fifty most common names in each part of the country, the fifty most common names in each decade from the 1890s to the 1970s, and names used for both men and women,
  81456298

Almqvist, E. J. R. *Ettusen nya svenska släktnamn.* Stockholm, Wahlström & Widstrand [1936]. 32 p.
CS2605 .A55

From page five: "Detta häfte har kollationerats med Svenska familjenamn 1920 jämte supplement till och med okt. 1935. Svensk namnbok, Lebergs Heraldiskt lexikon samt Finlands statskalender och adels kalender." One thousand surnames listed alphabetically with no further information.
  36033493

Blomqvist, Marianne. *Från tillnamn till släktnamn i österbottnisk allmogemiljö.* [Vasa]: Svensk-österbottniska samfundet, [1988]. 290 p. Ill., extensive bibliography, index.
CS2609 .P64 B57 1988

A dissertation from the University of Helsinki that "deals with the emergence and evolution of surnames from 1780 to 1930 in the rural Swedish speaking part of the province of Ostrobothnia in Finland . . . ." [p. 6]. Chapter five, " Tillnamnens innehåll och ursprung" [content and origin of surnames], pp. 134-211, lists many individuals and gives short biographies with family affiliations. Other chapters mention individuals in shorter lists. The bibliography, pp. 241-70, lists archives, manuscripts, and printed sources consulted. Index of all names discussed.
8148403

Carlsson, Albert W. *Vad betyder våra namn?* Stockholm: LT, 1980. 111, [1] p.

CS2605 .C37

Names taken from the "Almanack" (see Klintberg below), which lists first names in name-day order. The list is chronological with an alphabetical index at the end. Each entry gives a five-to-ten-line explanation of the name's origin, historical details, and the time from which it first appeared in the "Almanack." Some of the names go back to the seventh century and are pre-Christian.
80504796

Fredriksson, Ingwar. *Svenskt dopnamnsskick vied 1500-talets slut.* Lund: distribution, Inst. f. nordiska språk, Helgonabacken 14, 1974. 187 p.

CS2375.S8 F7

Baptismal names. The first one hundred pages present statistical tables of names and their occurrence geographically and chronologically. By perusing the tables, the researcher may be able to determine that a particular name was popular in only one geographical area in the sixteenth century. This can narrow down a search for an ancestor. The following seventy pages list names alphabetically, with the same kind of statistical information, as well as alternate forms when appropriate. Alphabetical index of all names occurring in the book. Bibliography of primary sources consulted.
75562960

Hjelmqvist, Theodor. *Förnamn och familjenamn med sekundär användning i nysvenskan: onomatologiska bidrag af Theodor Hjelmqvist.* Lund, C.W.K. Gleerup [1903]. xxx, [2], 411, [1] p.

CS2601 .H6

Pages 1-313, first names. Pages 314-53, surnames. Clear explanations of origins and meanings of names, geographical and chronological extent of use, whether foreign borrowings, dialect or of other non-standard origin. Gives alternate forms. No index nor bibliography.
09022839

Kjöllerström, Per August. *Svensk namnbok. Dopnamn, ättenamn, ortnamn.* Ulricehamn, S.M. Kjöllerström [1895]. 3 p. l., 175, [1] p., 1 l.

CS2601 .K5

Pages 1-96, baptismal names; pages 96-140, surnames; pages 140-74, place names. Separate lists of men's and women's first names arranged by origin, mostly geographical or ethnic. For first names some lists give a brief meaning, but most do not. Surnames are treated with origin and meaning, and listed according to their origin as foreign names, names taken from trades, or other. A unique feature

is the eight-page list of "grundord," i.e., foundation-words, that are the most frequent components of surnames and place names, with meanings given for each foundation word. No general index, which makes names difficult to find.
  09030673

Klintberg, Bengt af. *Namnen i almanackan.* 1. uppl. [1st ed.] [Stockholm]: Norstedts Ordbok, 2001. 452 p.

CS2375 .S8 K57 2001

  Names listed in name-day order with an alphabetical list at the end. Explanations of meaning and origin are approximately one page long per name.
  2002399800

Larsson, Inger. *Dåpp Inger, Tupp Lars och Jacobs Olof: om gårdsnamn i Nås socken i Dalarna.* Uppsala: Uppsala universitet; Stockholm: distributor, Almqvist & Wiksell, 1995. 82 p. Ill., maps, bibliography.

CS2607 .L37 1995

  In Dalarna, the use of the names of farms from which an ancestor once came (gårdsnamn) has entered written records and often become part of an official name consisting of farm name + first name + patronymic. This study involves primarily names occurring in the parish of Nås, covers the period 1680-1900, and few individuals can be identified, but a perusal of the book gives researchers in Dalarna records a better understanding of the names they may encounter. Six-page bibliography, no index, two-page summary in English.
  96133337

Lee, Ingmar A. (Ingmar Adelbert). *In search of Ingmar.* Minneapolis, MN: I. Lee, 1978. 16] p. Ill.

CS2608.I54 L44 1978

  A study of as many people named Ingmar as the author could find. Many individuals are listed and brief biographical, and sometimes genealogical, information accompanies them. There appears to be no order, and the only criterion for inclusion is that they share the author's first name. No index.
  80107787

Lidaräng, Arnold. *Lurel och Smesa: västgötska personnamn i muntlig tradition*; teckningar av Sven Björnson. Stockholm: I distribution hos LT,1982. 255 p. Ill., index, bibliography.

CS2609 .V37 L5 1982

  The use of nicknames in records is a phenomenon in West Gotland that apparently is found to a far lesser degree elsewhere in Sweden, and can, therefore, serve as an indication that the person who bears the name may be from West Gotland. This book studies the subject in detail, with much statistical information, and provides a very interesting insight into the practice. It also contains a twenty-seven-page alphabetical index of names studied and a five-page bibliography.
  82174359

Malmsten, Anders. *Svenska namnboken.* Stockholm: Rabén Prisma, 1996. 279 p. Bibliography.

CS2375 .S8 M35 1996

Basically a what-shall-we-name-the-baby book, this gives considerable information on each name: the date of the name day, the meaning and origin of each, its numerical place in the list of most popular names, and a unique set of arrows that indicate whether each name is increasing or decreasing in popularity now, and whether it has done so over a long period of time. Lists of the one hundred, 1,000, and 2,800 most popular boys' names and girls' names. A one-page bibliography.
97155943

*Personnamnsstudier. 1964: tillägnade minnet av Ivar Modéer (1904-1960).* Stockholm: Almqvist & Wiksell, [1965]. 344 p., [2] p. of plates, ill., map, single-page bibliography, indexes.
CS2601 .P47 1965

Eighteen articles by different authors. All are titled in both languages: Hard and Skrepp, some evidence for early farm names in upper Dalecarlia; Hypocorisms and bynames according to place of residence in the dialect of Anundsjö; Siunde and Skönnebol; Notes on some Scandinavian personal names in English 12$^{th}$ century records (in English); 500 years of Västergötland christian names; The man's name Løki and the place names Löckerum and Lokrume; The usage of patronymics combined with family names among the Swedish nobility; The runic man's name Haursi; Personal names in Upper Norrland place names; Nomenclature in the account book of a country shop keeper in Skåne; Fale and Falebro; The names in the Swedish calendar; From the oldest schedules of population from Norrbotten; Some medieval forms of the name Johan; Two names of Swedish provinces; On the name Rabbe; Dialect names in Swedish speaking Estonia; Alver and Ølver. Indexes of personal names, place names, and subjects. Each Swedish-language article has a summary in English
90174368

Sandström, Raija. *Finska och icke-finska tillnamn i Nedertorneås kyrkböcker på 1800-talet.* Umeå: Distribution, Institutionen för nordiska språk, Umeå universitet, 1985. xviii, 226 p., extensive bibliography.
CS2609 .N43 S26 1985

Surnames and place names from parish registers in Haparanda and adjoining rural districts. Much statistical material on occurrence and composition of names, meanings of Finnish forms, and Finnish names altered to fit Swedish phonology. No general index of names; names must be found in each section of each chapter. English-language summary on pages 261-65.
85223027

*Släktnamn i Umeå 1622-1820.* samlade och utgivna av Kungl. Vetenskapssamhällets Personnamnskommitté. Umeå: Kommittén: Distribution, Institutionen för nordiska språk, Umeå universitet, 1984. xxiv, 442 p.
CS2609 .U44 S54 1984

A doctoral dissertation on names in Umeå and its surroundings from 1622 to 1820. Four hundred and forty-one pages of surnames, listing every person who bore each name, with information on family and profession. A section of variant spellings of some of the names.
84229424

Sundqvist, Birger. *Deutsche und niederländische Personenbeinamen in Schweden bis 1420;*

*Beinamen nach Herkunft und Wohnstätta.* Stockholm, Almqvist & Wiksell [1957]. 442 p. Bibliography.

CS2605 .S8

Swedish personal and place names of German and Dutch origin, arranged alphabetically and exhaustively documented. Fifteen-page bibliography.
58025859

Thors, Carl-Eric. *Finländska personnamnsstudier.* Stockholm, Almqvist & Wiskell [1959]. 138 p.

CS2607 .T5

A ninety-eight-page, alphabetical list of surnames used through the 16th century in Finland. Some individuals are identified with personal details, but the study primarily locates names in times and places in both Finland and Sweden where further research may be fruitful; it also indicates the possible geographical origins of families. Each surname occupies approximately half a page, with citations for all sources.
67055465

United States. Central Intelligence Agency. *Swedish personal names.* [Washington] 1967. 46 p.

CS2605 .U5

A thirty-page list of given names and surnames with seventeen pages of prefatory material telling how Swedish names are formed and pronounced. Sketchy explanation of transliteration and pronunciation of Russian names in Swedish, Danish, Norwegian, Dutch, Icelandic, and English.
68061074

Washington, D.C.
February 2006

Made in the USA
Las Vegas, NV
27 November 2023